Winner of the American
Institute of Physics
Science Writing Award,
Early Childhood News
Directors' Award, and
Parents' Choice
Approved Award

ISBN-13: 978-0-8249-6798-7 (softcover)
ISBN-10: 0-8249-6798-4 (softcover)

ISBN-13: 978-0-8249-6799-4 (hardcover)
ISBN-10: 0-8249-6799-2 (hardcover)

Library of Congress Cataloging-in-Publication Data
Hauser, Jill Frankel, 1950-
Science Play! : beginning discoveries for 2- to 6-year olds / Jill F. Hauser
p. cm. – (Little hands : 9)
Includes index.
Summary: Contains sixty-five activities that introduce readers to scientific exploration, including such subjects as weather, soil science, plants, color, and light.
               (alk. paper)
1. Science—Study and teaching (Elementary)—Activity programs—juvenile literature. 2. Science—Experiments—Juvenile literature. [ 1. Science—Experiments. 2. Experiments. I. Title. II. Series: Little hands (Charlotte, Vt.); 9
Q164.H33 1998
507' .8—dc21
97-39475
CIP
AC

*Little Hands*® Series Editor: Susan Williamson
Illustrations: Michael P. Kline/Michael Kline Illustrations
Design: Georgina Chidlow-Rucker

Published by Williamsonbooks
An imprint of Ideals Publications
A Guideposts Company
Nashville, Tennessee
www.idealsbooks.com
800-586-2572

Printed and bound in Singapore
10 9 8 7 6 5 4 3 2

# Science Play!

By
Jill Frankel Hauser

Illustrations by
Michael Kline

### Beginning Discoveries for
### 2- to 6-Year-Olds

## williamsonbooks™
Nashville, Tennessee

## Dedication

To my mother, Maxine Frankel, for instilling in me a profound respect for learning, seeking out the best growing experiences L.A. had to offer, and for giving me my precious first activity book!

## Acknowledgements

Thank you Laurie and Don Burk, committed scientists and parents both, for your sensitive technical review. Special thanks to my class of kindergartners at Rother Elementary School for the zest with which you plunge into and consume the knowledge science yields.

# williamsonbooks™

### by Jill Frankel Hauser

## Super Science Concoctions

50 Mysterious Mixtures for Fabulous Fun

## Kids' Crazy Art Concoctions

50 Mysterious Mixtures for Art & Craft Fun

## Gizmos & Gadgets

Creating Science Contraptions that Work (& Knowing Why)

## Wow! I'm Reading!

Fun Activities to Make Reading Happen

# CONTENTS

# For Kid Scientists ...

Would you like to make friends with an earthworm? How about creating a flipping elf? Or would you like to make awesome sound-gizmos for a one-kid band? If you like to slosh water, smush mud, balance on one foot, or just quietly observe the critters outdoors, then you'll love the huge variety of exciting science activities that awaits you.

Some activities you can do on your own. For others, ask for the help of a grown-up lab assistant. And best of all, many activities are fun to try with a friend. For hours of hands-on science fun, you've come to just the right place!

## Safe Science

- Taste only with a grownup's permission. In this book, look for this symbol which means "OK to eat!"

- Wear an apron or old clothes for messy activities.

- Have a grownup be your laboratory assistant and get permission before experimenting.

- Use only plastic containers for experiments. Make sure all equipment is clean and dry. Wash after use.

- Keep your hands away from your mouth and eyes while experimenting. Wash your hands with soap and water after each experiment.

- When outdoors, observe but don't disturb.

- Help yourself to samples from nature only if you have permission and if it is no longer alive.

- Bring along a backpack—and a grownup (no wandering off by yourself).

- Everyone helps clean up when you are finished.

For Kid Scientists and Grown-Up Lab Assistants

7

# and Grown-Up Lab Assistants

What do little kids and rocket scientists have in common? They carefully observe their world, then wonder, "Why?" And that's what scientific thought is all about! Cook in the kitchen, or garden in the backyard. If a child is nearby, you'll be bombarded with observations and questions.

"Where does rain come from?"

"Yikes! It's a big bug!"

"Why are you putting in milk?"

While you may not have all the answers, you can offer experiences that help to figure things out. With your guidance, squirting water, collecting rocks, and watching insects become the beginnings of scientific thought.

## You're Never Too Young To Think Like a Scientist

Although scientists use complex laboratory techniques to make discoveries, their first observations are much the same as a child's. What textures, colors, sounds, or smells can you observe? Which trees have broadleaves, which have needles?

*Gathering and organizing information are core science skills.* They're skills information-hungry kids practice naturally and enthusiastically. All children need are their own world to explore and your science spin on their thinking. There's biology in the backyard, chemistry in the kitchen, and physics in the block pile!

## Science Skill Builders

Science skills that boost thinking ability and help children make sense of their world are embedded within each activity in this book. Here they are listed for you to apply anytime, anyplace.

**Observe.** Although seeing is how we often define observation, it's only one information-gathering tool. Encourage children to use all their senses for observing. How does the rain sound? Can you smell those beautiful flowers on the desk? How does the taste of milk change after you mix in the cocoa? Compare the feel of sand with the feel of soil.

**Explore.** Free exploration makes the best introduction to science. Invite children to plunge containers to the bottom of the sink or tour the lawn with a magnifying glass. Exploration also involves experimenting with variables. What happens when you add blocks to only one side of the tower? What happens to the mud pie when you add sand? What happens to a top when you lengthen its tip and shorten its handle?

**Communicate.** Kids need to know how to express their observations and ideas. Using science words makes them feel grown-up. New vocabulary is best learned informally in the context of talking with you about their discoveries. Words influence thought. For example, learning the words "broadleaf" and "evergreen" can open up a whole new way of looking at neighborhood trees and categorizing information.

**Organize.** There are many ways to organize information.

> **Compare and match.** How are these sounds alike? Different?
>
> **Order and sequence.** Can you put these rocks in order from tiny to large? Light-colored to dark? Smooth to rough?
>
> **Sort and classify.** Organizing collections is a wonderful way to sort and classify. Display found treasures thematically: leaves, seeds, or finds from a particular location or season.

**Record.** Information becomes more valuable when recorded and shared. Recording allows kids to build on past learning. Other folks can share the discovery and add their insights. Not only can children sketch or dictate, they can wiggle like an earthworm or act out growing like a seedling.

**Apply science.** Young children learn about technology when they apply science to everyday events. Once you discover that staying in the shade protects you from the bright sun, you might be inspired to invent portable shade for wherever you go!

For Kid Scientists and Grown-Up Lab Assistants

9

# Scientific Method for Little Learners

Asking questions and finding answers is so important to scientists that they've developed an organized way to do this. It's called the scientific method. Try a science experiment together like Garbage Viewer on page 19. Or next time you're asked a question, simply invite the child to follow these easy yet powerful steps for discovering the answer:

**Look and ask.** Pick up on an observation your child makes that inspires a question: "My Popsicle is awfully messy." "Why does icy stuff get so drippy on a hot day?"

**Guess.** Ask your child to guess why it's so. "I think the sun melts it."

**Test.** Create an experiment and put the guess to a test. "Let's see what happens when we put one ice cube in the sun and one in the shade." Carefully observe and keep track of what happens. "Both cubes are melting, but the one in the sun is all watery now!"

**Find out.** What conclusion can a child make based on the test? How did his guess fare? "Just as I thought. The sun must have melted the ice because the one in the shade isn't all the way melted yet!"

**Look and ask again.** The wonderful part about the scientific method is that finding answers leads to more questions and the whole process starts again! Help children apply what they learned to generate new questions and tests: What makes shade? What happens to a chocolate bar in the sun? Can I cook with the sun?

*"Guess, Test, and Find Out"* is an easy way for children to apply the core of the scientific method to everyday wonders. It's also a refrain you can use to address all their puzzling questions. You'll empower children with the skills needed to get closer to the answers on their own!

## Science Supplies

All activities in this book use safe, inexpensive household or easy-to-find materials. The right collection of stuff becomes an exploration-lab for open-ended play and experimentation. In some activities, your backyard or schoolyard becomes an exciting learning place. Other activities simply put a science spin on everyday events making science an integral part of every child's life. After all, science for little kids is all about discovering their world!

***Here are some of the items you'll need and where to find them:***

**Grocery Store:** Salt • Sugar • Cornstarch • Flour • Gelatin • Food coloring • Liquid dishwashing soap • Cooking oil • Chocolate chips • Borax

**Craft Store:** Art paper • Tempera and watercolor paint • Markers • Pipe cleaners

**Around the House:** Measuring spoons and cups • Soda straws • Mixing container and spoon • Water • Plastic storage containers with lids • Coffee filters • String • Waxed paper • Clear soda pop bottles • Resealable plastic bags • Medicine dropper • Tape • Newspaper • Cereal box cardboard • Clear film canisters • Ice cubes

# Home, Sweet Home

The earth is more than a place for people; it's every creature's home, too! Look outside. Do you see plants and animals that share our home on earth? Get to know these plants and critter friends. It's a good time to explore and polish your observation skills, to be on the look-out for wildlife, and to think about ways we can each make our earth home a better place for us all. If you love being outdoors, the activities ahead are just for you!

11

# Science Safari

## Science Safari

Go on a walk with an attitude—a science attitude, that is! Scientists look carefully at the world around them. By *observing*, they make amazing discoveries that can make the earth a better place to live. You can be a scientist, too. Take a science safari right in your own backyard. What do you *see*, *hear*, *smell*, and *feel*? Don't forget your backpack. You'll want to carry important "finds" from the "field" back to your at-home "laboratory."

## Color Walk

Bring a box of crayons on this nature safari and hunt for twigs, leaves, or petals to match each color. Don't forget the sky, critters, and earth, too. Which crayons have the most matches? These are the colors of your world! Use them to draw a picture of what you saw. Take a color walk each season, and see how the colors change.

## Sound Search

Don't say a word on this walk. Just keep your ears open for sounds. Can you hear wind rustling, birds singing, or leaves crunching? Try this search on your porch on a summer's night. Are night sounds different than day sounds?

## Touch Tour

Hunt for interesting things to feel: smooth leaves, craggy rocks, and rough bark. Place a sheet of paper over flat finds, and use the side of a peeled crayon to rub textures onto the paper.

## It Makes Scents

Sniff the air as you take this hike. Bring home small samples of fragrant leaves and flowers. Back home, place each sample in a clean, catsup squeeze bottle. Squeeze and sniff. Can you remember which plant smelled this way?

## Wet Walk

Grab your boots and raincoat to take a science safari after it rains. Stomp in puddles and in slithery mud. Feel shiny leaves. Stand under a drippy tree. How did the rain change your world?

QUACK!

## Plant World

Explore the plant world. Gather treasures lying on the ground that are no longer growing. Ask a grownup to make you a couple of masking tape bracelets. Wear them sticky-side out. Then inspect bark, seeds, leaves, stems, flowers, weeds, and twigs, and stick tiny treasures on your bracelets.

## Bug Hunt

You may have to crawl like a bug to find these tiny critters. Carefully lift rocks, stir leaf piles with a stick, or dig into the soil to discover bugs and their homes. Crouch down and watch awhile, using a magnifying glass.

Home, Sweet Home

13

# Mini-Museum of Interesting, Strange & Wonderful Treasures

What can you do with your many science safari treasures? Pick out favorites and sort them into mini-museums. How about showcasing items found in the same place or habitat by color, season, kind, or size?

## 12 Tiny Treasures

An egg carton makes a display for tiny finds.

## Shoe Box

Holds smaller, labeled containers (resealable bags, clear film canisters, clear deli containers).

## Nature Mobile

Wind yarn among the branches of a stick. Hang your collection from the web of yarn.

## Stick-it-on Bands

Snip open the sticky bracelets described on page 13. Tack the bands on a wall to display.

## Clay Display

Make Quick Dough by mixing together ½ cup (125 ml) salt, 1 cup (250 ml) flour, and ½ cup (125 ml) water. Press pebbles, seeds, and dried weeds into a flattened dough ball. Leave them in the dough, or remove them and save their prints.

**Read It!**
Are you a good observer? Read and see. *I Spy* riddle books by Jean Marzollo, *Look! Look! Look!* by Tana Hoban

# Nature Notebook

The best way to learn about nature is to observe very carefully. How can you remember your amazing discoveries? How can you share them with a friend? Record your discoveries in a nature notebook!

## HERE'S WHAT YOU NEED:

- Notebook with blank pages
- Pencil or pen
- Crayons, markers, or colored pencils
- Paste, tape
- Small, resealable plastic bags

## HERE'S WHAT YOU DO:

There are many ways to note your discoveries, as you observe and record.

### Nature Treasures

Paste interesting finds into your notebook. Leaves, feathers, twigs, seeds, pinches of soil or sand can be saved in small, plastic lunch bags and taped to a page.

### Sketch It!

Draw what you see: an insect, a plant, or a cloud. Scientists use arrows to point out details in their drawings. Sketch a bug and then draw arrows to label legs, wings, or other parts.

Home, Sweet Home

## Tell What, When, and Where

Have a grownup help you date and label each entry. Then dictate where you were. State the weather or an interesting fact: "May 30. My backyard. It is windy."

## Talk About It

Ask a grownup to write down your words as you tell about what makes your treasure special or how you found it.

## Helping Hands

Scientists communicate and share their discoveries by recording their findings. The process of sketching the specimen is what's important, not how realistic the picture looks.

Grownups should write exactly what the child dictates. The process of writing about what one sees is what's valuable and exciting.

Kids can write, too. Early writing may look like scribbles, letter-like shapes, or attempts at "grown-up" words. Celebrate all efforts to observe and record like a scientist!

# Circle of Earth

Who lives in your community? Police officers, grocers, kids, grandparents, and many more folks. Wildlife that lives together creates its own *community*. Find an outdoor observation spot. You may be surprised at the natural community of wildlife right outside your door!

## HERE'S WHAT YOU NEED:

• 5 feet (1.5 m) of string

## HERE'S WHAT YOU DO:

**1.** Knot together 5 feet (1.5 m) of string into a large loop.

**2.** Go outside and find an interesting patch of earth to explore. Encircle the spot with the string and mark it off with pebbles.

**3.** Crouch down low or lie low on your tummy. Look carefully at your little circle of earth. Can you see more close-up than you saw at first glance? Do you see bugs? Plants? How many different kinds? Is your spot shady or sunny? Is it near bigger plants, out in the open, or in sidewalk cracks?

Home, Sweet Home

# Bug Hotel

Planet Earth is home for you and your family. Who else makes Earth its home? Meet and observe some of your tiniest neighbors by inviting them to spend a night at the Bug Hotel.

## HERE'S WHAT YOU NEED:

- Hand shovel
- Empty cottage cheese or yogurt container
- Stones
- Board
- Apple or cheese

## HERE'S WHAT YOU DO:

**1.** Dig a small hole in a spot where bugs like to visit. Set the container in the hole so its rim is level with the earth. Add a bit of cheese or apple and a few leaves to attract guests.

YAY!

**2.** To make a safe roof, set stones around the edge of the container and place a board on top.

**3.** Check the hotel each morning to see what guests have arrived. Gently empty the container into a plate or pan. Sketch each critter in your Nature Notebook before setting it free. Notice how many legs, wings, eyes, and body parts it has. Observe what it eats, too.

# Garbage Viewer

One way to think about garbage is this: wherever garbage covers the ground, that's one less place for wildlife to live. What happens to the garbage at the dump? Does it disappear? Or does it stay around? *Guess*, *test*, and *find out* by burying some garbage in your garbage viewer.

## HERE'S WHAT YOU NEED:

- 2-liter soda bottle
- Lettuce leaf
- Garden soil
- Apple slice
- Styrofoam

## HERE'S WHAT YOU DO:

1. Have a grownup cut off the top and punch holes in the bottom of a 2-liter clear soda bottle. Hold a lettuce leaf against the plastic wall as you fill the bottle with dirt from your garden. Slip in an apple slice and a piece of Styrofoam packaging along the other sides of the bottle.

2. Set the bottle on a pie plate. Spray soil as needed to keep it moist.

3. Mark a calendar the day you set this up. How many days until the lettuce or apple makes a change? How does the Styrofoam look on this day? What did you find out?

**Read It!**
Read about how critters clean up their town in *The Great Trash Bash* by Loreen Leedy. It's also in Spanish: *Cura el mal de la basura!*

Home, Sweet Home

# Make a Splash!

It sloshes. It splashes. It flows and spreads. It can even change its shape. What is this amazing substance? Why, it's water! With a grownup's assistance, fill a sink, bathtub, or wading pool with water. Now start the science fun by exploring the wonderful ways of water!

**Note:** Never play around water without a grownup's help. Even if you know water safety rules, your friends and little sisters and brothers may not know them.

# Changing Shapes

An amazing quality of water is that it takes on all sorts of shapes—from the shape of your favorite cup to the shape of a swimming pool. Pour some water into a plastic resealable bag. Seal the bag; then slosh it around in your hands. See how it flows and changes shape? Here are ways to explore more shapes this funny stuff called water can take.

## Deep To Shallow

Collect different-shaped bottles and bowls. Look for tall, thin ones and flat, shallow ones. Pour a cup of water from one into the next. Does the water take the shape of each container?

## Make a Mist

Fill a spray bottle with water and squeeze the trigger. Compare the shape of the mist to the water in the bottle.

## Jug To Cups

Fill a gallon (4 L) jug with water. Pour it out into cups. How many cups of water did the jug hold?

## Fat To Flat

Pour a jug of water onto a driveway. What shape is the water now?

## Drippy Droplets

Dip your hand in water. What shape is water at the tip of each finger?

## Silly Shape

Fill a rubber glove with water. Use a twist tie to seal. What does the water look like now?

# Solids and Liquids: What's the Difference?

Something very special about water and other liquids (things that move like water—like a milkshake) is that *liquids flow to take the shape of their containers*. Did your explorations show you this was true?

Well, next experiment with something *solid*, like a rock. Set it in some of the containers you used to test water. Does the solid rock flow to fill the container? Does it change its shape? So, what's the difference between solids and liquids?

**Read It!**
Read *Water Dance* by Thomas Locker to see water in many beautiful places in nature.

# Super Fun
## Go on a Liquid Shape Hunt

Look for liquids throughout the day: water in the bathtub, juice in the pitcher, milk in your glass. There are so many liquid shapes! How do they change? Now search for solid shapes: books, computers, and trees. They're everywhere!

## Guess The Liquid

Can you drink it? Is it white? Does it come from a cow? It's milk! Your friend can ask up to five yes-or-no questions to try to guess the liquid you are thinking of. You can also play "Guess the Solid."

# Wiggly Water Necklace

Explore the marvelous ways water moves. Will water wiggle? Will it stop flowing once it begins to move? Wear some for awhile and see!

## HERE'S WHAT YOU NEED:

- Clear film canister
- Water
- Crayons
- Blunt knife
- Glitter
- Duct tape or waterproof adhesive tape
- Paper clip
- String

## HERE'S WHAT YOU DO:

**1.** Fill the canister ¾ full with water. Add a pinch of glitter. Add a pinch of crayon bits made by scraping a crayon with a blunt knife.

**2.** Ask a grownup to help you seal the top; then attach a paper clip with thin strips of duct tape. Thread the clip with string, and knot the ends together so that you can wear it around your neck.

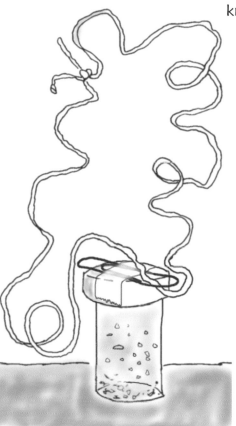

Make a Splash!

# TEST IT OUT!

Put on your canister necklace. Jump, hop, and walk. Does the water wiggle? How does it move?

Freeze your necklace. Does the water move? How did it change? Then wear it and move about. What can you do to make it wiggle again?

# Wonderful Water—
# Solid and Liquid!

It's amazing, but water can be both a solid and a liquid! Try this: fill a small, empty yogurt container part way with water. Can you slosh it around? Does it take a new shape when poured into a different container? Yes! Liquids flow and take the shape of their containers. *So the water is a liquid.*

Now place that cup of liquid water in the freezer until it is frozen hard. Can you still slosh it around? Place the chunk of ice into a different-shaped container. Does the solid ice take on a new shape like liquid water? Of course not! Solids are rigid and keep their own shape. *That's what solid water is like!*

Make a Splash!

25

# Wonder Water Bottles

Use clear plastic soda bottles to make these amazing water movers and cool bathtub toys!

## Stop-and-Go Flow

Ask a grownup to make a hole in the bottom of a bottle. Also make one hole in the center of the lid. Fill with water. Tighten the lid. Hold your finger over the hole in the top. Does the water flow from the hole beneath? Lift your finger. What happens now? Amazing!

## Jet Squeeze

Ask a grownup to poke five holes, about ¼" (5 mm) apart in a horizontal (across) row near the bottom of a bottle. Fill it with water. How many water jets do you see? Fill the bottle with water again. This time "squeeze" the jets together with your fingers. How many are there now?

## Compare the Spurts

Ask a grownup to poke three holes, widely spread apart, in a vertical (up and down) line along the side of a bottle. Fill the bottle with water. Compare the spurts. Which hole spurts the longest jet? The shortest?

> **TIP FOR GROWNUPS:** Here's an easy way to punch holes in plastic. Hold a nail with pliers. Heat the nail over a candle.

# More to Explore

*Compare* some of the many ways water can *move*. Which are the fastest ways, slowest ways, and your favorite way of moving water?

**Rock** water back and forth in a sealed plastic soda bottle.

**Blow** across the surface of water in a bowl. Use a straw to blow beneath the surface of the water.

**Pour** it on the driveway.

**Spray** water from a spray bottle.

**Squeeze** water from a squeeze bottle.

**Shoot** water from a garden hose.

**Drip** water from your fingertips.

**Spill** water from a jug onto the sidewalk or driveway.

**Splash** water with your hands and feet in a tub or pool.

Make a Splash!

# Nature's Movers

Most of the earth is covered with water—water on the move, that is. If you've been to the beach, you've seen ocean water lapping against the shore. Have you ever seen a waterfall or a spring? Moving water is all around us as part of our natural world.

**Observe nature carefully for water on the move.** Do you notice a leaf moving with the water in a creek? Just as you can blow across the surface of a bowl of water, the wind blows across the surface of the ocean, making waves. Streams (currents) also flow throughout the ocean moving vast amounts of water from place to place. What happens to raindrops as they land on a window? Can animals make the water move in a still pond? Can you make water move in a lake?

KAPLOOP!

# Floaters and Sinkers

Will it float? Will it sink? Make good predictions and hope your choices don't go kerplunk when dropped in water. You might win the game!

## HERE'S WHAT YOU NEED:

- Bowl of water
- Floaters and sinkers such as paper clip, pebble, leaves, small toys, bottle cap, comb, ping pong ball, lump of clay

## HERE'S WHAT YOU DO:

1. Prepare the game by filling a deep, clear bowl with water (with a grownup's supervision). You and your friend have just 5 minutes to gather 12 objects you *predict will float*.

2. Take turns testing each object. Does it float or sink? Place tested objects in floater or sinker piles. Count your floaters. The player with the most floaters is the winner. Or play cooperatively. Both players win if most of their collection of objects are floaters!

Play the game again, but this time gather a new collection of objects you think will sink. The winner will be the player with the most sinkers!

Set a lump of modeling clay in water. What happens? Can you mold it into a shape that floats?

Make a Splash!

29

# Super Fun

Make icebergs for a warm bath or wading pool. Freeze water in milk cartons. Unmold by setting the cartons in the tub for a few moments. Dump the cubes into the tub. Do they sink or float? Is more of the iceberg below water or sticking out on top? How have the giant ice cubes changed by the end of your bath?

Imagine an ice cube over 100 miles (160 km) long and several hundred miles deep, floating around in the ocean. Such giant "ice cubes" really do exist! Scientists call them *icebergs*. Icebergs look huge when you see them, but what you see floating is only a small part of the ice. Most of the iceberg is hidden from view, deep beneath the sea.

Icebergs can float about freely. Some are found hundreds of miles from where they were first formed. What can you do with icebergs? Scientists have thought about shipping them off to dry countries to use as a source of fresh water. Now that's an interesting idea!

# Get Soaked!

What would you use to sop up a spill? What material would make a good raincoat? Play this game by predicting which materials soak up water and which materials don't.

## HERE'S WHAT YOU NEED:

- Medicine dropper
- Cup of water
- Objects for discovery such as plate, foil, waxed paper, paper towel, cotton ball, T-shirt, jeans, wood, magazine, cardboard, newspaper, leather shoe, tennis shoe, rock, leaf, sponge.

## HERE'S WHAT YOU DO:

You and your friend have 5 minutes to gather 12 objects you *predict will soak up water*. Line up these objects on the floor.

1. Use a clean medicine dropper or your finger to drip a few drops on to each object, one at a time.

2. Lie on your tummy and view each drop from the side. *Does it form a dome shape or does it disappear?* If a dome forms, it means the material doesn't soak up water very well. The water just sits on top. The winner is the player with the most objects that *absorb* (soak up) the water drops so they will disappear.

Make a Splash!

# More to Explore

## Predict!

This time collect objects you *predict will repel* (keep away) the water like a raincoat does. You don't want the water to soak into these items. The winner is the player with the most objects that make the water form little domes. What material would make the best raincoat (repel)? How about the best towel (absorb)?

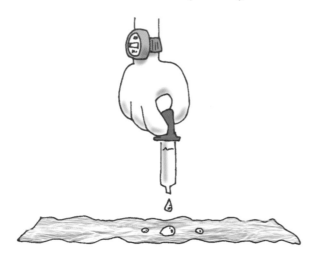

## Feel It!

Get a knit mitten and a plastic bag. Place your hand in the plastic bag. Plunge your hand into a tub of water no further than the top edge. Now put on the mitten and take the plunge. Which got you wet (absorbs the water) and which kept you dry (repels the water)?

# Super Fun

## Penny Challenge Games

**Drops on a penny.** Set a penny on a plate. *Predict* how many drops of water can fit on a penny. Use your medicine dropper and start dripping. Count and see if you were right. Get your eyes at penny level. What shape is the water?

**Pennies in a cup.** Set a cup on a plate and fill it to the rim with water. How many pennies do you *predict* you can add to the cup before the water spills over? Count and see if you are right. Get your eyes level with the rim. Check out that amazing bulge!

## How can a Sponge Hold So Much Water?

It's all those tiny holes for the water to fill. Look closely at your socks or a towel with a magnifying glass. Can you see places for water to be stored? That's why a towel works so well for drying you off and why a sock can absorb sweat from your feet. Now look at a plastic plate or the kitchen countertop. No holes there for water to fill, so a splash of water sits on top in little domes instead, waiting for you to sop them up.

# Water Designs

Here are two science facts that add up to artistic fun!

- **Water moves in wondrous ways.**
- **Paint is mostly made of water.**

Now take what you know about liquids (water) and explore fun ways to move paint into beautiful designs.

## HERE'S WHAT YOU NEED:

- Water
- Watercolors
- Tempera paints
- Crayons
- Marble
- Spoon
- Straw
- String
- Paintbrush
- Art paper
- Bowls

*Make a Splash!*

# HERE'S WHAT YOU DO:
## Marble Tracks

Set your paper in the bottom of a deep bowl or box lid. Drop a marble in a cup of tempera paint. Use a spoon to lift out the marble and place it on the paper. Tilt the bowl or lid back and forth. Try more colors. *What do you observe?*

## Air Painting

Place spoonfuls of watery tempera on paper. Try blowing them into interesting shapes with a straw.

## Crayon and Paint

Draw a picture with crayons. Now paint over the entire picture with watery paint. What do you notice about where the paint soaks in? Where does the paint form tiny domes?

## Drag It!

Set a string in a bowl of paint and place it on a sheet of paper. Fold the paper in half, sandwiching the string inside. Press down on the paper as you drag the string side-to-side and pull it out. Use new string for each color.

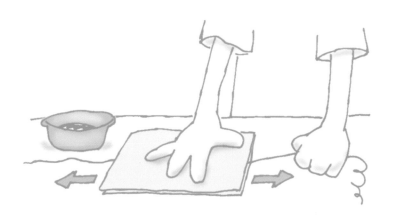

## BLOT IT

Fold a sheet of paper in half and open it again. Place small spoonfuls of paint near the fold. Refold the paper. Use your palm to push the paint outward. Open up the paper to see your work of art.

## FUZZ OUT

Dip paper in water. Drip drops of watercolor paint here and there. What happens to those colorful puddles?

## Your Way!

Can you think of your own way to move watery paint across paper?

Make a Splash!

35

# Air, Air Everywhere

Although you can't see air, it's everywhere. Look for clues. Put your hand in front of your nose and breathe hard. What do you feel? That's air that has traveled through your body and helped keep you alive! Look outside. Are trees swaying or is laundry flapping on the line? That's caused by air on the move, called wind. The activities in this section show you how to look for air-is-there clues, capture air, and even put it to work!

# Is Air There?

You can't see air, but if you observe carefully, you'll know it's there. Watch for clues. Discover air by exploring the amazing things it does.

## Puffy Pillow

Make tiny scraps of tissue paper confetti and place them in a resealable plastic bag. Seal the bag closed against a straw. What happens in the bag when you blow through the straw? Now quickly pull out your straw and zip it shut. What shape is the bag now? What makes it so puffy? What made the paper fly?

## Science at Work

Crumple a paper towel and jam it into the bottom of a glass. *Predict* what will happen if you push the upside-down glass straight down into a tub of water. Try it and see. Were you right? It seems like magic that the towel is dry, but really it is science at work. What do you think kept the towel dry?

## Press on Power

Stand up and press a sheet of paper to your tummy. Let go. What happens? Now press a sheet of paper to your tummy and run forward. Let go. What happens? What do you think is holding the paper up?

Air, Air Everywhere!

# Book Drop

Tear up scraps of newspaper and spread them out on the floor. Drop a book on top of them. What happens to the scraps? What made them fly?

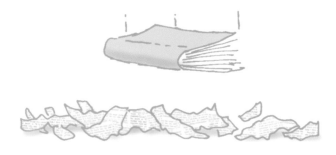

# Bag It

With a grownup's help, hold the handles of an open plastic grocery bag and run with it. Twist it shut and hold on to the top. Pat and squeeze the bag. Why do you think it feels so fat and squishy? Squeeze the air out slowly so it hits your face. How does it feel?

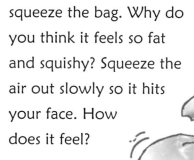

# Catch It

Ask a grownup to help you flap a sheet up and down. What makes the sheet stay up high for a few moments? What makes it puffy?

# Helping Hands

Air is everywhere, but since it's invisible it's hard for little ones to know it's there. These activities allow children to observe the effects of air's presence. Gradually, they will realize that the invisible air is what is common to all of these activities.

**Read It!**

To learn more about air, read *The Air Around Us* by Eleanor Schmid.

# I'LL Huff and Puff

The big, bad wolf did lots of damage to piggy homes with his huffing and puffing. But maybe the wolf should have used a straw to blow those houses down! See how powerful your puffs of air are—with and without a straw.

## HERE'S WHAT YOU DO:
### Fabulous Straws

Blow on your hand. How does it feel? Now blow through a straw onto your hand. Does the air feel different? When your breath is forced into the narrow space of a skinny straw, it moves very quickly. This gives your breath great strength. It becomes powerful enough to move objects clear across the floor.

## HERE'S WHAT YOU NEED:

- Straws
- Toy car
- Plastic jar lid
- Tape
- Various small objects to test

*Air, Air Everywhere!*

## Investigate

For each of these tests, blow on objects through a soda straw. *Collect* all sorts of objects. Set them along a starting line (in front of a string or stick placed on the ground). *Predict* which one will go the farthest with just one puff. Get predictions from family members, too. Now use your straw and your breath to *test and find out*.

## Invent a Winner

You and a friend each take ¼ of a sheet of paper. Bend, roll, crumple, tear, cut, or fold it anyway you like to make the "blowing-est" thing possible. Mark a start and finish line. Set up your creations. Point your straws. Ready, set, blow, and go!

# Sail Away

Punch 2 holes in an index card. Weave a straw through to make a sail.

**Sailboat:** Tape the straw against the inside edge of a plastic jar lid. Float the boat on water. Try to move it with your breath.

**Sail car:** Tape the straw to the back end of a small toy car. Set the car on a smooth surface. Try to move it with your breath.

Tape here →

# Water Drop Race

Set a piece of waxed paper on the table. Draw start and finish lines at each end. Using straws, can you and a friend blow water drops across the race course?

# Sucking Up Cereal

Fill a bowl with dry puffed cereal. Can you figure out how to move the cereal from one bowl to another using a straw?

*Air, Air Everywhere!*

## Blast Off

Tear off one end of the paper wrap around a straw. What do you think will happen when you blow from the torn end? (Make more blasters by rolling small paper tubes. Fold over and tape the tip.)

## Salt Dune

Place a few spoonfuls of salt on a pie pan. Can you change the shape of the salt mound by blowing through your straw?

## What On Earth?

Put moving air and loose sand together and what do you have? A majestic sand dune. Dunes can be huge—as large as a building. Sand dunes keep growing as long as the wind keeps blowing. The wind causes the sand grains to move in different ways. Some grains "jump." Larger grains "creep" and "roll." Sometimes the wind even causes the sand to "hang" in the air like a cloud.

# Fan and Roll

Test the power of moving air by putting it to use. Can you think of a way to scoot a toy from one end of a room to the other without ever touching it? Set air in motion and see what happens!

## HERE'S WHAT YOU NEED:

• Paper
• Tape
• Marking pens

## HERE'S WHAT YOU DO:

**1.** Decorate two sheets of paper to make a colorful toy. Fold one sheet, accordion-style, into a fan. Roll a 2" x 5" (5 cm x 12.5 cm) strip from the other sheet into a tube. Hold the tube together with tape.

**2.** Can you use your fan to roll the tube? Have your friend do the same. Play an air-powered racing game by seeing who can fan and roll their tube from a start to finish line across the room.

*Air, Air Everywhere!*

43

# Super Fun

**Make another air-powered toy with newspaper.** You and your friend each cut a page of newspaper into a large shape. Simple shapes like whales or bats work well. Use a book to fan your shape across the room. Can you keep your shape from touching the floor? What do you think causes the shape to move?

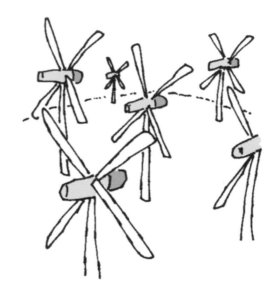

## What On Earth?

### Air Power!

Moving air is powerful stuff. In nature, moving air is wind. Wind energy is clean and free. What a wonderful source of power! Just as you observed how moving air can scoot a toy across the floor, creative inventors have discovered ways to put the power of wind to work.

For hundreds of years, windmills have used the power of the wind to grind grain into flour and pump water from one place to another. Today, we can capture even more wind power with many windmills spinning at the same time. These wind farms look like fields of mechanical flowers.

# Air Spinners

A piece of paper is a wonderful piece of scientific equipment. Use it to be an *explorer* and *experimenter*. Your job is to create a paper spinner that catches the air and hovers for awhile. Compare the different ways these air spinners move. Which stays aloft the longest?

## HERE'S WHAT YOU NEED:

- Paper
- Safety scissors
- Tape

## HERE'S WHAT YOU DO:
### Spinning Bar

Cut a 5 ½" x 1" (14 cm x 2.5 cm) strip of paper. It's easy to snip it from a quarter sheet of paper. Hold it high and let it go. Observe the action.

- Make different-sized strips.
- Cut strips from different kinds of paper.
- Fold up each end about ½" (1 cm).

TIP: For the best spinning action, start your spinners as high up from the ground as possible. Stand on a stool for a good launch.

*Air, Air Everywhere!*

## FLipping FiSh

Cut a 1" (2.5 cm) strip from the short edge of a sheet of paper (8 ½" x 11" or 21 cm x 27.5 cm). Snip each end as shown. Connect it together at the snips so that it looks like a fat fish. Hold it high and let go. How does your fish move?

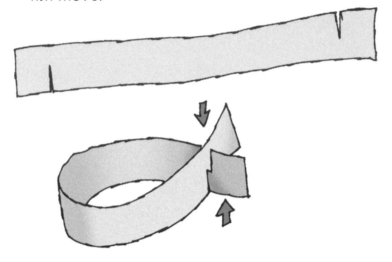

- Make different-sized strips.
- Cut strips from different kinds of paper.
- Pinch the nose or leave it rounded.

## TwirLing TriangLe

Cut out a 2" x 5 ½" (5 cm x 14 cm) rectangle. Make 2 cuts as shown and tape the ends together. Toss high in the air and watch how it spins to the ground.

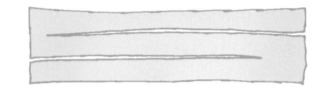

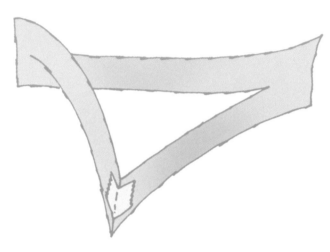

- Start with different-sized rectangles.
- Cut rectangles from different kinds of paper.
- Use a paper clip instead of tape to hold it together.

# More to Explore

## Target Practice

Can you predict where your spinners will land? Set a wastebasket on a mat. Place this "target" at the edge of a sofa. Take turns with your friends dropping spinners from the sofa. Give yourselves 2 points for landing in the bucket and 1 point for landing on the mat. Which type of spinner lands most often in the bucket?

**Read It!**

Join Henry the cat on a sky-high adventure in *Hot-Air Henry* by Mary Calhoun. Or read *Flying* by Donald Crews.

## What On Earth?

The seeds of the maple tree are little spinners. Their special shape lets them spin gently to the ground very much like the Twirling Triangles. Why do you think spinning seeds are good for maples? Because the seed spins slowly to the ground, there's more time for the wind to carry it away—perhaps to a wide-open space with lots of sunlight!

Which, of all the creations on pages 45–46, do you think makes the best spinner? Which stays in the air the longest? Which moves out the farthest? Which makes the gentlest landing?

*Air, Air Everywhere!*

# Go Fly a Kite

How can an ordinary sheet of paper rise high in the air and stay there? Change that paper into a kite. Let air push against it in just the right way and—it flies! Be an aerodynamic engineer (someone who designs airplanes) and as you build your kite, test it along the way.

## HERE'S WHAT YOU NEED:

- Sheet of 8 ½" x 11" (21 cm x 27.5 cm) paper
- Tape
- Scissors
- Drinking straw
- Newspaper
- Kite string
- Rubber band
- Crayons or markers

## HERE'S WHAT YOU DO:

**1.** Fold a sheet of 8 ½" x 11" paper in half. Make a diagonal fold across the rectangle. Now fold each wing of the kite along that fold.

**2.** Tape along the fold to hold it together. Tape a drinking straw across the top of the kite from wingtip to wingtip. There's your kite shape! Toss it into the air. What happens?

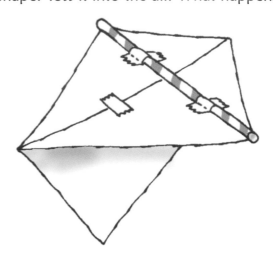

**3.** Punch a hole in the center fin right where it lies on the straw. Attach about a yard of kite string or thread to the hole. Attach a rubber band handle to the other end. Tape on a tail of one or two columns of newspaper.

# Test It Out

Hold onto the string with one hand. Hold the kite high in the air with the other. Let the kite catch a gentle breeze as you let go of it and tug on the string. What's happening? Compare this action with the tossing action in step two, page 48. What do you think makes the difference?

No breeze? Hold onto the rubber band handle and run. Glance back at the kite. What's happening? Hold your kite while you stand still. Now what happens to the kite? What do you think it takes to make a kite fly high in the air?

Air, Air Everywhere!

49

## Drag It!

What did you observe as you held the string? Did you notice a tugging feeling? In fact, to get your kite going, you probably tugged at the string. You're actually pulling the kite against the air. Scientists call this *drag*. It's one of the forces that must be at work for your kite to stay up. What happened when you stopped feeling the tug? Your kite started dropping toward the ground! So do kite flyers like drag? You bet!

## What On Earth?

They are mostly flown just for fun, but kites have also been a help to scientists. Benjamin Franklin threaded a key onto his kite string during an electrical storm. His dangerous kite experiment taught the world about electricity. (Never fly a kite in a storm or add metal objects to a kite, of course.) Kites have also helped meteorologists (weather scientists) study weather.

# Sun, Wind, and Rain

Weather is always changing. That's why it's so much fun to watch. It changes from day-to-day and season-to-season. It even changes from hour-to-hour. Say, "How's the weather?" to a friend who lives across the country and the answer might surprise you! On the same day, the weather can be quite different in different parts of the country. Get ready to explore changes in the weather. Splash in puddles and wonder how they vanish. Play with the light and warmth of the sun. And feel the strength of the blowing wind.

# Sunny Day Shadow Play

A sunny day is perfect for exploring all sorts of shadows! Houses, cars, and trees all have shadows—and so do you! Keep track of your shadow for several hours. How does it change? Compare your shadow shapes throughout the day while you're standing still or walking.

## Me and My Shadow

In the morning, stand in an open area with your back toward the sun. Ask a friend to draw around your feet with a piece of chalk and then outline your whole body's shadow. Stand in your chalk foot outline at noon and again later that afternoon. Each time ask a friend to trace the outline of your shadow with a different color chalk. Ask a grownup to label each outline with the time of day. When does your shadow disappear?

7 am   Noon   5 pm

# Sunny Sun Visor

Is it one of those wonderfully hot and sunny days? A sun visor shadow is handy for protecting your face from bright sunlight.

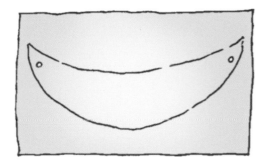

1. Ask a grownup to copy this pattern's shape onto a piece of construction paper. Cut it out. Since the sun will shine down on your visor, decorate it with sunny designs.

2. Reinforce the holes with tape. Thread with string and adjust to your head. Wear your visor in the sunshine. Is your face in the sun or the shade? Does the visor's shadow move as you walk?

# Shadow Games

Does your shadow go where you go? Does it move the way you move? Play these shadow games and find out!

## Shadow Tag

"It" must tag another player's shadow with her own. Then that person becomes "it." The game ends when everyone has been tagged.

## Shadow Safe

Have one person shout, "Go!" To be safe, you and your friends must step on other kids' shadows. When "Stop" is called, freeze. If you're not standing on a shadow, you must sit down. The winner is the last player left standing.

## Shadow Creature

Make a shadow shape with your body. Have a friend add his shape to yours. Now add another. Have one person outline the entire shape with chalk. How many heads, arms, and legs does your creature have?

Sun, Wind, and Rain

## Shadow Art

It's not just big things like the human body and trees that cast shadows. Even the smallest items cast a shadow—a spider weaving a web casts a moving shadow. Look outside for little shadows: shadows of flowers, branches, or grass. Try to catch the shadow on paper held in a clipboard. Use a pencil to outline the shape. If you like, color in the shapes back at home.

## Shadow Show

Cut animal and people shapes from lightweight cardboard. Tape a stick (ruler, branch, or paint stirrer) onto the shape for a handle. Find a sunny wall and you're ready for a puppet show. Hold up your creatures so they block the sun and let their shadows tell a tale.

# More to Explore

Learn more about shadows from your Teddy bear. In a dark room:

- Shine a flashlight *near* your bear. Can you make it look really big?
- Shine your flashlight *far away* from your bear. How does it look now?

## Shadow Lengths

As the earth spins, the sun seems to move across the sky. When the sun is low in the morning and evening skies, shadows are long. When the sun is high in the midday sky, there are no shadows or they are very short.

MORNING SUN

MORNING SHADOW

## Let's Get Practical

- Sit in the shade of a tree or building. Now sit in a sunny spot. Compare how you feel in each place.
- Predict what happens to an ice cube set in the shade and one set in the sun.
- If you have a pet cat, notice where he sits during different times of day. Why do you think he likes those spots?
- Brainstorm ways to feel cool on a hot, sunny day.

Sun, Wind, and Rain

# Wind Sock

How do you know the wind is there? *Feel* it blow through your clothes and hair. *Listen* to the sound trees make as they sway in a breeze. On a windy day, *watch* what happens to clothes on the line or piles of fallen leaves. Use a wind sock to help you make wind observations.

## HERE'S WHAT YOU NEED:

- Brown paper lunch bag
- Newspaper
- Magazines
- Paste
- Scissors
- Two 20" (50 cm) lengths of string

## HERE'S WHAT YOU DO:

**1.** Cut the bottom from a paper bag. Decorate the bag collage-style by pasting on bits of color or interesting words and pictures from old magazines.

**2.** Cut out column strips from the newspaper. Paste these streamers onto the bottom edge of the bag so that they dangle all around.

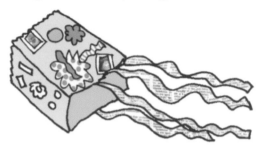

**3.** Ask a grownup to help you reinforce two spots across from each other on the top edge with tape. Punch a hole in each spot. Thread the string through the holes and knot the ends in place. Tie another piece of string to use as a handle and hanger. Hang outside your window where you can watch the wind's action.

Check your wind sock for signs of wind. Listen for rustling. Look for fluttering. Is there lots of wind or just a little breeze? What direction does the wind seem to be coming from? Check again in a few hours. Has anything about the wind changed?

# More To Explore

Hold your wind sock string and run. Can you make it flutter even on a calm day?

Paste newspaper streamers across the back half of a paper headband. Now run through the wind! How do you feel? How do the streamers sound?

The world's first weather vane was a wet finger! That's right, so hold yours in the air. Feel which side dries first. Let this observation tell you where the wind is coming from.

## What On Earth?

Winds can tell you a lot about the weather. If they come from the ocean, they might be carrying rain. If they come from the land, they might be warm and dry. North winds are usually cold. Winds can actually bring weather all the way from a faraway place—right to your own backyard!

**Read It!**
Curl up with a good book on a windy day!
> *One Windy Wednesday*
> > by Phyllis Root
> *Millicent and the Wind*
> > by Robert Munsch
> *The Wind Blew*
> > by Pat Hutchins

*Sun, Wind, and Rain*

# WeT WorLd

Rainy days can be filled with fun—especially if you're allowed to go outdoors and play in the rain. That's the best way to learn about rain—get out there with the raindrops!

## Rainy Day Safari

Grab your , raincoat, and a willing grownup. Now go out for a  in a gentle rain. How do  sound on your ? How do drops feel on your ? Does the  look different when it's wet? Has the color of the  changed? Are different  out and about? Does the air have a special smell? After the  stops, feel the slippery 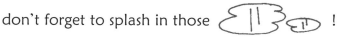 and muddy soil. And don't forget to splash in those 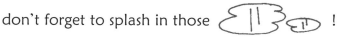 !

## Pitter Patter Band

If the sound of rain is music to your ears, try this. Make a band by placing hollow containers in the rain: upside down metal coffee can or pie plate, plastic milk jug placed on its side, cottage cheese container with lid, plastic stretched over a can and held in place with a rubber band. Compare the different sounds and rhythms of rain.

# More To Explore

## Pitter Patter Paint

Let the rain help you paint a picture. Use tempera to paint some splotches or stripes on a piece of paper. Set the dry painting outside for a minute on a rainy day (not too long or you'll end up with a soggy paper). What happens to the tempera? Look at your raindrop painting, decide what it looks like, and give it a name—Dancing Dots by Raindrops.

## Raindrop Landing Pad

Mix 1 cup (250 ml) flour with ½ cup (125 ml) salt. Fill a pan with about a half-inch (1 cm) of this mixture. Hold the pan in the rain for a few seconds to catch a few drops. Wait a few hours; then use a fork to carefully lift out the doughy wet spots. Set them on a plate in a warm place to dry. What shapes are raindrops: balls, or blobs, or egg-shaped ovals? Arrange your drops in order from tiny to huge.

## Measure The Rain

It is fun to keep track of the weather by predicting it ("Looks like rain with all those dark clouds") and by measuring what actually happens. You may be surprised when you compare how much rain actually falls in a brief, heavy rainfall as compared to a long, gentle rain.

### Here's How:

Set a ruler inside a straight-sided, clear jar. Use a permanent pen to mark and number level lines in inches or centimeters. Set the jar in an open area on a rainy day. Push pebbles around the bottom of the jar so it won't tip over. Check, record, and empty the water after each rainfall.

Sun, Wind, and Rain

59

# Cloud-in-a-Bag

Make it rain with the magical ingredients of soil, moisture, plant life, and heat.

## HERE'S WHAT YOU NEED:

- Soil and small plants
- Plastic resealable bag
- Spoon
- Water

## HERE'S WHAT YOU DO:

**1.** Take a few spoonfuls of damp soil from your yard, along with a few small plants like grass. Carefully lay the soil and plants in the bottom of the bag. Add a spoonful of water to the soil without getting the walls of the bag wet. This is your *mini-earth*.

**2.** Seal the bag tightly and tape it to a sunny window. What do you notice happening inside the bag? See how cloudy it looks? That's a *mini-cloud* forming. See the drops along the walls of the plastic? Those are *mini-raindrops*. Tap on the outside of the bag and many of those tiny drops will come together. Watch how they form drops heavy enough to fall back to the earth. You've created a *mini-rainstorm*!

# More To Explore

## Be a Water Droplet Detective!

Observe carefully and you'll see water droplets forming all around you.

- Drink ice-cold water on a warm day. Check the outside of your glass.
- Take a warm shower. Check the mirrors in the bathroom.
- After a cool, clear night, check the leaves of a plant in the early morning.

## Let's Get Practical

The puddles you see on a rainy day will soon become rain again. If that sounds like magic, it's not—just pure science at work! Here's what happens:

- As water warms in the sun, it changes to vapor (a gas, like air). It rises high in the sky.
- The water vapor cools and forms clouds of water droplets.
- When the droplets become heavy, they fall to the earth as   you guessed it—rain!

Sun, Wind, and Rain

# Puddle Prints

Explore your own mini-puddles to discover how rainy day puddles disappear. Let the sun change colorful puddles into pretty print designs.

## HERE'S WHAT YOU NEED:

- Watercolors (mix food coloring with a little water)
- Plastic page protector or reuse clear, rigid plastic packaging
- Medicine dropper
- Hole puncher
- Yarn
- Scissors

## HERE'S WHAT YOU DO:

**1.** Use a dropper to drip watercolor puddles onto the plastic. When you like the puddle pattern, carefully set the plastic in the sun. What do you think will happen?

**2.** Let the puddles dry. How did the sun change your puddles? Cut the colorful plastic into simple shapes. Punch a hole at one end. Thread the shape with yarn and hang in the window. Let sunlight shine through your pretty puddle patterns.

# What On Earth?

Puddles are everywhere on a rainy morning. But if the sun comes out, are they still there by afternoon? Keep track of the action on your driveway or sidewalk by drawing the outline of a puddle's edge with a piece of chalk. Make new outlines every half hour or so. What's happening to your puddle? Compare the difference in how quickly puddles disappear on hot, cool, and windy afternoons.

# Super Fun

Paint or draw in watery ways on your driveway or sidewalk. How do your wet pictures change after a while? What do you think made them disappear?

## Water Paint

Use a small brush and a bucket of water to paint a picture.

## Squeeze Art

Squirt water out of a squeeze bottle in an interesting pattern.

## Icy Art Stick

Freeze water in an empty frozen orange juice container. Then peel away some of the cardboard. Use your icy art stick to draw on concrete. What happens to your art stick?

Sun, Wind, and Rain

# Weather Watch

Be a meteorologist (weather scientist) by keeping a careful watch on the weather and recording what you observe. Find out which times of year are cold, rainy, warm, or windy.

## HERE'S WHAT YOU NEED:

- Large calendar
- Colored pencils

## Read ALL About IT

Ask a grown-up to share the newspaper's weather report with you. You'll find a prediction for the day's weather. Was it correct?

## Dress for The Weather

How will you dress for a sunny, snowy, rainy, or windy day?

## Think just about Hats

What kind of hat keeps the sun off your face yet lets the cool air through? What kind keeps your head warm and can't be blown off by the wind? Which hat keeps you dry in the rain? If you could have just one hat, which kind is most important where you live?

## HERE'S WHAT YOU DO:

1. Be a meteorologist. Keep track of the weather on a calendar at the same time every day. Draw symbols for the weather on each square: sun, cloud, raindrop, snowflake, or kite for wind.

2. Have a grownup help you read a thermometer and record the temperature in the corner of the square.

| SUN | MON | TUE | WED | THU | FRI | SAT |
|---|---|---|---|---|---|---|
| | 1 60° | 2 62° | 3 57° | 4 55° | 5 54° | 6 54° |
| 7 59° | 8 60° | 9 58° | 10 60° | 11 62° | 12 64° | 13 |
| 14 | 15 | 16 | 17 | 18 | 19 | 20 |
| 21 | 22 | 23 | 24 | 25 | 26 | 27 |
| 28 | 29 | 30 | 31 | | | |

# Super Fun

What better way to report the weather to your family than to look like the weather of the day!

- Make a basic headband.
- Decorate.
- Trace around an 8" (20 cm) plate on cardboard. Cut it out.
- Trim about 2" (5 cm) off the bottom, making a shape a little larger than a semi-circle.
- Cut away the center, leaving a 1 ½" (3.5 cm) headband.
- Round the inner corners.
- Trim away more as needed to fit.

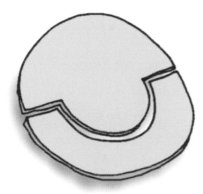

## Sunny

Paste on yellow triangle-shaped rays. Wind thin strips of yellow paper on a pencil to make curled streamers. Paste them on and shine!

## Cloudy

Paste on white cloud shapes to be a floating cloud.

## Rainy

Paste on gray cloud shapes. Add curled gray streamers at each side for rain.

## Windy

Make the wind headband on page 57. Run to make your streamers blow.

Sun, Wind, and Rain

## Stormy

Make the rainy day hat. Paste on lightning bolts. Using long strips of cardboard, make large lightning bolts you can hold in your hands.

## Snowy

Paste on paper snowflakes. Add white curled paper streamers at each side.

# More To Explore

**Dance.** Place your hat on your head and dance like the day makes you feel. How does a wild storm, the bright sun, or softly floating flakes make you want to move?

**Listen** to *The Four Seasons* by Antonio Vivaldi. He wrote music to match the seasons of the year. Can you guess which season you are listening to?

**Read It!**
Read these books about weather and seasons: *Seasons on the Farm* by Jane Miller, *Anno's Counting Book* by Mitsumasa Anno, *The Year at Maple Hill Farm* by Alice and Martin Provensen.

# CeLebRate PLaNTS

Even if you live in the heart of a city, when you look outdoors, you'll likely see plants. From giant pines to tiny grasses growing in sidewalk cracks, plants live all around us. And that's a good thing, because we couldn't live without them. All of our food comes from plants (or from animals who eat plants). Plus, plants help give us oxygen to breathe. Here you'll grow plants from seeds, make crafts with flowers and leaves, and even befriend a tree. Learn about our growing, green friends as you celebrate plants!

# pebble PLanT?

Is a pebble alive? Is a bean alive? Sketch what you *predict* will happen when you add a little water to each. *Guess, test, and find out* as you carefully observe a living thing grow. It's really amazing!

## HERE'S WHAT YOU NEED:

- Pebbles
- Dried beans
- Water
- Jar
- Paper towels

## HERE'S WHAT YOU DO:

**1.** Soak a few different kinds of beans in one container and pebbles in another overnight. How have they changed by morning?

**2.** Layer 2 paper towels together, and fold and roll them. Push the roll into the jar so that it stands upright and touches the walls of the jar. Add enough water to wet the roll.

**3.** Push several different kinds of beans down between the paper towel roll and the jar on one side. On the other side, push down a few pebbles.

**4.** Think like a scientist by drawing a picture of what you *observe* now and another picture of what you *predict* will happen to the beans and the pebbles. Look at them everyday. Add more sketches of any changes you see. Compare with your prediction sketches. Were you right?

# Super Fun

## Bean Dream

Glue a bean to a sheet of drawing paper; then draw an amazing or silly thing sprouting from your bean. How about a dinosaur, a castle, or a new kind of plant?

## Bean Bottle

Beans are beautiful—and there are so many kinds! Make a bean bottle paperweight by filling a clear plastic jar with layers of different kinds of dry beans.

# More To Explore

## Which Way's Up?

If you studied your bean sprout carefully, you first noticed a tiny root pushing downward. Then you saw a shoot pushing upward. It's amazing that these plant parts "know" which way to grow! How "smart" is your bean plant? Test it and find out by starting another bean growing in a jar. When the root is about 1" (2.5 cm) long, screw the jar lid on tightly. Turn the jar upside down. Wait a few days and check. Now which way do you predict the root and shoot will grow?

## What's a Seed?

The beans you planted are seeds; the pebbles are not seeds and thus don't grow. A seed is a neat little package that holds a baby plant and its food. The tough outside coat protects what's inside.

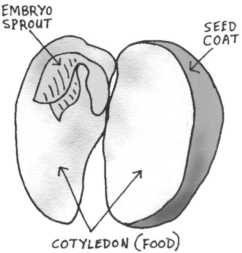

EMBRYO SPROUT

SEED COAT

COTYLEDON (FOOD)

Soak large beans like lima beans overnight and see if you can find these seed parts. The *seed coat* should soften and peel right off. Split the seed in half. Can you find the baby plant or sprout? It's called an *embryo*. The rest of the seed is the plant food called the *cotyledon*. If you like eating beans, then you like plant food, too.

Celebrate Plants

# Seedy Sock Walk

Seeds are in so many places. They seem to travel everywhere. Explore one way seeds move from place to place by going on a seedy sock walk!

## HERE'S WHAT YOU NEED:

- One large sock that fits over your shoe (ask a grownup)

## HERE'S WHAT YOU NEED:

1. Pull an old sock over your shoe. Ask a grownup to take you on a walk through a field of dry grass and weeds.

2. Back home, carefully pull all those seeds off your sock, sorting them into different piles as you go. If you have a magnifying glass, look closely to see the different seeds and try to *discover* how those seeds hook onto your sock. Count the different kinds of seeds you found.

# More To Explore

## Search Indoors

Here's a clue: there are seeds in the fruits and vegetables you eat. Ask a grownup to help you open an apple, orange, melon, peach, cucumber, winter squash, tomato, and more! Check out dried beans, popcorn, and raw peanuts, too.

## Eat Them

You won't need socks for your indoor seed safari, but a good appetite comes in handy! Make a fruit salad from the cut-up fruit. Add sunflower, poppy, or sesame seeds.

## Sort Them

A magnifying glass is helpful for observing details of seeds in your collection. Can you think of a way to sort them? How about by size, color, or shape?

## Plant Them

Place folded, moistened paper towels in a resealable plastic bag. Add a variety of seeds from your seed collection. Tape the bag to your window. Watch the action over many days. Do all the seeds sprout into seedlings?

Celebrate Plants

# Super Fun

Glue dry seeds and weeds onto paper for a lovely nature collage.

- Gather dried weeds on a nature safari. Back home, arrange them in an interesting way in a vase.

- Play nut memory by gathering 6 pairs of nuts. Set each nut beneath an upside down paper cup. Each player turns over 2 cups on a turn. If the nuts match, keep them and take  another turn. No match? Replace the cups. Now it's the other player's turn.

**Read It!**
*Pumpkin, Pumpkin* by James Titherington shares the wonders of planting a special seed. Eric Carle takes you on a seed's travels as you read *The Tiny Seed.*

# Helping Hands

What's the *difference*? What's the *same*? Ask these questions as kids examine their seed collections. A simple question often gets the *sorting* and *categorizing* process going.

# Movers & Shakers

Many seeds are made to travel away from their first home. A wide open field gives them plenty of space and sunlight to grow.

- Some seeds, like burrs, *hook* onto your pants or socks.
- Others, like dandelions, *float* gently to the ground with fuzzy parachutes or float on water like tiny boats.
- Some *twirl* to their growing spot like Air Spinners (see pages 45–47).
- Animals and insects are helpful seed movers, too—like ants who *carry* and *bury* seeds beneath the earth!
- Squirrels *gather* nuts, acorns, and other tree seeds then bury them to eat in winter. Sometimes they forget where they're stashed. Good thing for the buried seeds. In spring, they can sprout into trees!

# My Favorite Tree Book

Do you keep a scrapbook all about you? There might be pictures of you and souvenirs from important events inside. You are so special! Trees are special, too. So why not make a scrapbook to record all you learn and love about your favorite tree?

## HERE'S WHAT YOU NEED:

- White paper
- Construction paper
- Yarn
- Crayons
- String
- Scissors
- Tape
- Paste

## HERE'S WHAT YOU DO:

**1.** Assemble a book made of white paper pages and construction paper covers. Punch holes in the papers and tie the pages together with yarn.

**2.** Draw a picture of your tree. Ask a grownup to help you make these science labels: root, trunk, branches, leaves, bark. Paste these word labels next to each part. Add little arrows pointing to each tree part.

## Mark of The Bark

How does the bark feel? Make a bark rubbing by holding paper on the trunk and rubbing it with the side of a peeled crayon. Compare rubbings from other trees. Why do you think the bark is rough?

## Buds

For fun, ask a grownup to cut a twig or branch with buds from a tree in late winter or early spring. See what happens when you leave the cut end in a vase of water for several weeks. Sketch before and after pictures in your book.

Celebrate Plants

## Seeds, Pods, and Fruit

Tape flat seeds and pods into your book. Sketch fruit that comes from trees—apples, oranges, cherries.

The roots must cover a huge area to get enough water and minerals for the tree to live. Stand with your feet together. Now stand with your feet apart. Have a grownup try to gently push you over. Which way do you feel stronger? Can you think of another reason the tree's roots spread out so far underground?

## Flower Power

All trees bloom. Does your tree have showy flowers in the spring? If so, lay them between sheets of paper. Press them under the weight of several books for a few weeks. Then paste them into your tree book.

## Roots

You can't see them, but they reach out as far as the branches of the tree. Without this important part, the tree would fall over, dry up, and die! What part of the tree could this be? The roots!

## Friends

Who lives in the branches in your tree? On the trunk? Near the roots? On the leaves? Use a magnifying glass to help you find out. Sketch the animals and insects who make your tree their home.

## My Tree and Me

Why do you like your tree? Think about ways trees are wonderful and helpful. Here are some special things about trees: shade, animal homes, wood for building, paper for writing and drawing.

## Super Fun
### Make a Model of Your Tree

Roll two sheets of construction paper together. Snip up from the bottom and down from the top of the tube in several places. Gently pull out the strips to form roots and branches. Paste the roots onto a cardboard base. Use scraps of colored paper to fill the branches with leaves of the season. Is it autumn? Find orange, red, or yellow paper for leaves. Is it winter? No need to make leaves at all! What colors do you need for the leaves of spring and summer?

**Read It!**

Sit in the shade of your tree and enjoy looking through your tree book throughout the year! Enjoy these great books as well: *When Dad Cut Down the Chestnut Tree* by Pam Ayres, *The Giving Tree* by Shel Silverstein, and *A Tree is Nice* by Marc Simont.

Celebrate Plants

75

# Leaf Celebration

Leaves come in so many shapes, colors, and sizes. Get to know the leaves in your neighborhood by collecting, sorting, and saving them. Just remember, whatever their size or shape, all leaves do the same thing. They are the amazing food-makers for the tree. Hooray for leaves!

## HERE'S WHAT YOU NEED:

- Leaves
- Crayons
- Paint
- Construction paper
- Paste

## HERE'S WHAT YOU DO:

Use a plastic bag to collect all kinds of leaves. Sort them into piles by:

**Shape:** feather, hand-shaped, oval

**Edge:** saw-toothed, scalloped, smooth

**Texture:** fuzzy, slick, leathery

**Number on a stem:** several or one

**Size:** large, medium, small

**Shades of green:** from light to dark green

**Autumn colors:** yellow, red, brown, orange.

## WHAT DO LEAVES DO?

All those veins in your leaves give you a good clue! Leaves are busy food factories. Water and minerals travel through those veins all the way from the tree's roots to the uppermost leaves! Leaves also take in air and sunlight. They use those ingredients to make plant food, called sap. Sap also travels through those veins to nourish other parts of the tree. Now do you know why the branches hold those leaves high in the sky?

## Leaf for Keeps

Sandwich your favorite freshly picked leaves between sheets of white paper, then newspaper. Be sure they do not touch each other. Place heavy books on top and wait about two weeks. Now hang them on the refrigerator, around windows, or add them to your tree book (page 73), if they come from your tree or one of its neighbors.

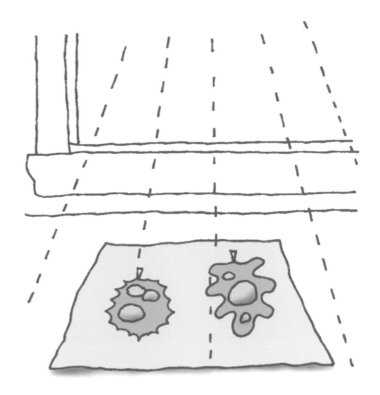

## Mail Away

The trees in your neighborhood are probably different from those in a friend's neighborhood in another state or province. Why not exchange pressed leaves (protected by shirt cardboard)?

## Sun Prints

Place a sheet of construction paper in a sunny spot. Use small rocks to hold leaves in place on top of the paper. Wait several hours. Lift off the leaves. What do you see? Why do you think this happens? (Hint: colors fade when left in the sun.)

## Leaf Match

The wind can blow autumn leaves far from their parent tree. Sort out a few leaves from a pile. Can you find the tree they came from?

Celebrate Plants

# 3 Kinds of Leaf Prints

**1.** Paint the vein side of a leaf with tempera paint. Press it gently onto paper. This print makes a neat greeting card.

**2.** Press the vein side of a leaf into a flattened ball of play dough or soft clay. Remove the leaf. Let dry for a record of your leaf.

**3.** Place a leaf, vein-side up, under a sheet of paper. Peel the paper from a crayon. Rub its side over the paper. Voila! Your leaf appears, veins and all.

# Autumn Crown

Collect autumn leaves before they turn crisp. Carefully pinch off their stems to use as "thread." Overlap the leaves. Hold them in place by "stitching" in and out with the stems.

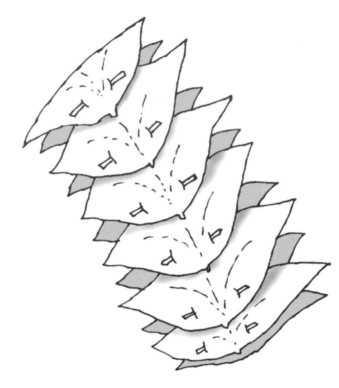

**Read It!**
Read *Red Leaf, Yellow Leaf* by Lois Ehlert. Are you inspired to plant a family tree?

# Flower Power

Flowers use colors and fragrances to "welcome" insects. You can use flowers to make lovely crafts. Explore the sweet smell and colorful sight of flowers.

## HERE'S WHAT YOU NEED:

- Variety of fresh flowers, leaves, blades of grass
- Sheet of thick cardboard
- Cotton cloth: white sheet, pillowcase, or handkerchief works well
- Wooden mallet
- Dowel
- String

## HERE'S WHAT YOU DO:

**1.** Place fabric on top of a sheet of cardboard on the sidewalk.

**2.** Plan an interesting color pattern using leaves, petals, whole flowers, and blades of grass on one half of the fabric. Fold over the other half to make a flower sandwich.

**3.** Now the fun part! Use a mallet to pound the colors from the plants.

**4.** Open the fabric. Remove the plant parts. You've made a lovely banner design of natural colors. Ask a grownup to staple the top edge of the cloth to a dowel. Attach ends of string to each dowel tip. Hang to display.

Celebrate Plants

79

## Stationery

Decorate paper the same way you made the colorful fabric to make bookmarks, greeting cards, and stationery.

## Potpourri

Not only are flowers colorful, they smell good! Sniff out the best-smelling flowers in your yard. Or ask a florist for some sweet-smelling flowers that have wilted. Pull off the petals and place them in a shallow bowl. Dry for several days in a cabinet. Store dry petals in a jar with a tight-fitting lid. To use, place a handful in a small bowl for all to enjoy.

## Let's Get Practical

**Why so colorful and fragrant?** It's a flower's way of inviting special visitors to stop by. Many plants need insects, birds, and bats to help make their seeds. When a visitor, like a bee, drinks nectar from a flower, the bee gets dusty from the flower's *pollen* (the yellow powder in the flower). As the bee travels from flower to flower, pollen from one flower brushes onto a special part of another flower. This must happen for seeds to develop. Insects just can't resist a flower's lively color, fragrant scent, and sweet nectar. Good thing for those flower fields!

# Down To Earth

Look closely at the ground, and you are very likely to see rocks. Some are colorful and others are not. Some are huge and others are tiny. Huge boulders, large stones, pebbles, and sand are simply different-sized pieces of rock. The breakdown of rocks gives us rich soils and dirt that we just can't live without. How else would plants grow to feed us and our animal friends? So, get your hands into mud, start a rock collection, and build with sand and soil. You'll discover the wonderful world of earth beneath your feet.

# Inside DirT

Pick up a lump of soil and squish it between your fingers. What's it made from? Explore the soil around your home by actually taking it apart!

## HERE'S WHAT YOU NEED:

- Soil
- Water
- Spoon
- Small clear plastic jar with lid

## HERE'S WHAT YOU DO:

1. Put a few large spoonfuls of soil into a small jar.

2. Slowly add enough cold water to almost fill the jar. Seal with the lid.

3. Shake, then wait. What do you see? Part of the soil floats to the top. Part of the soil sinks. Why do you think this happens?

## What On Earth?

You can find soil in so many places. Where does it all come from? Your jar of soil and water gives you a clue.

Rocks are worn down over time by rain and wind breaking them into smaller and smaller pieces. You see these tiny bits of rock at the bottom of the jar. Soil is also made up of tiny bits of dead plants and animals. This is what you see floating to the top.

Put together these bits and pieces of long ago and you've got the soil of today right in your own backyard!

# Worms at Work

Busy as a worm? Yes, these wiggly creatures work hard making garden soil rich. Invite some to visit your own worm farm for a few days, and watch the action. Observe carefully and you'll learn about the neighbors who live beneath our feet.

## HERE'S WHAT YOU NEED:

- Large clear jar
- Dark cloth
- Soil
- Sand
- Leaves
- Earthworms

## HERE'S WHAT YOU DO:

**1.** Carefully fill a clear plastic jar with three wide layers of soil and two thin layers of sand (soil, sand, soil, sand, soil). Spray each layer with water.

**2.** Now look for some worms willing to visit your farm for a few days. Mark the spot where you found them with a marker flag. Assure the worms of a speedy release after you watch them hard at work.

**3.** Place a few worms in the jar. Cover with a layer of dead leaves. Remember, earthworms live in the dark underground so cover the jar with a dark cloth to make them feel at home. Set the jar where it will not be too warm, too cold, or disturbed.

**4.** Check on your guests after a few hours and then each day. See what happens to your neat layers of soil and sand. Then return your guests to where you found them.

Down to Earth

# More To Explore

Be a zoologist and gently put worms to the test!

## Moving Along

Observe carefully. How do worms move? They squeeze and stretch, squeeze and stretch, eating their way through the soil. Can you squeeze and stretch your way across the floor?

## Listen Closely

Bristles on earthworms' bodies help them grip and move. Use a magnifying glass to see the bristles. Now try to hear them at work. Place a worm in a paper cup or paper bag. Put your ear close. Listen for a scratching sound.

## Light or Dark?

Shine a flashlight on the worm for a second. What does it do?

## What's for Dinner?

Offer your worms tiny bits of leaves, grass clippings, vegetables, and fruits. Which do they pull into their burrows first?

Worms can't live for long in a jar. Please return them to the earth, exactly where you found them, after a few days of observation.

# Super Fun
## Transform Your Finger into a Worm Puppet

Line a small box top with brown construction paper or with a color photo of dirt. Ask a grownup to poke a finger-size hole through the lid. Now poke your finger through the hole and wiggle it like a worm! To make the worm home look even more real, fill the lid with leaves or dirt.

## What On Earth?

## What Has No Eyes, Breathes Through Its Skin, and Eats Soil?

The earthworm! Earthworms are so helpful. They make great soil for growing plants. A garden full of earthworms is a wonderful thing. That's because earthworms pass tons of soil through their bodies. They drag humus into their burrows, making the soil rich. They bring air and water to plant roots as they tunnel around. What hardworking creatures!

**Read It!**
Read about your underground friends in *Wonderful Worms* by Linda Glasser.

# Earth Pies

You can't eat them, but by mixing up concoctions for mud pie and sand pie, you'll learn about these important earth materials. Think like a scientist and compare how they are alike and different. *Question* why they crumble. *Investigate* ways to make them stronger.

## HERE'S WHAT YOU NEED:

- Clean, fine soil
- Clean, fine sand
- Water
- Shovel

## HERE'S WHAT YOU DO:

**1.** Add just enough water to the soil until it sticks together.

**2.** Pat a scoop of wet mixture between your hands and squeeze. Gently set the pie to dry in the warmth of the sun.

**3.** Now try steps 1–2 using sand in place of soil. Compare the dry pies. Which can you pick up without it crumbling?

Which makes the better earth pie—sand or soil?

## More To Explore

A well-made earth pie holds together. Which kind of mixture makes the best pie? Oozy, gooey, gritty, mushy? Change amounts or add new ingredients and see what happens.

- Change the amount of water. Is the pie too crumbly or too gooey?
- Change the type of soil or sand. Try using different kinds around your yard.
- Add sand and soil to the same pie.
- Add leaves or twigs.
- Add grass clippings or straw.
- Which stuff makes the best pie?

Down to Earth

# Super Fun

## Mud Pot

Make a mud ball. Now poke your thumb into the center. Press it until it becomes shaped like a pot.

## Mud Prints

Flatten a mud pie. Press your hand or your foot or even your elbow into the pie to make a print. Next try an object like a leaf.

# Mudland and Sandland

Mold wet sand or soil into a castle or town. A line of sticks can be a fence. Pebbles can form paths. Plant cuttings stuck in the dirt can be tiny trees and bushes.

## What On Earth?

### Listen To The Story

Sand is simply incredibly tiny rock! Take a look at a pinch of sand under a magnifying glass. Each grain has a story. The round smooth grains were probably smoothed against an ocean shore or riverbank. Or maybe they've traveled long and far. The grains with sharp edges are young by sand standards. They probably broke off more recently and haven't had a chance to become smooth. Listen to the sounds of the earth. Rub a pinch of gritty sand between your thumb and forefinger near your ear. Try again with fine, smooth soil. Can you hear the difference?

### Read It!

Imagination mixes with mud in *The Mud Pony* by Caron Lee Cohen. Then read *Sand Cake* by Frank Asch. Do you love exploring mud and sand as much as this little bear?

Down to Earth

87

# PIES FOREVER

Ask a grownup to mix 1 cup (250 ml) of cornstarch with ¾ cup (175 ml) of water in a pot. Heat slowly, and stir until the mixture looks like gravy. After it has cooled, knead a spoonful of this cornstarch glue into about a cup (250 ml) of sand or soil. Make simple shapes, creatures, or castles with the earth goop, and let them dry hard.

# Brickworks

An ordinary mud pie will just wash away in the rain. *Guess, test, and find out* how you can make it strong enough to be used to build a house. In some parts of the world people have done just that. With some guessing and testing, builders figured out what to add to mud (like you did on page 85) to turn it into a strong *adobe* brick. Why not give it a try?

## HERE'S WHAT YOU NEED:

- Soil (fine clay soil works best)
- Water
- Dry grass clippings or straw
- Hand shovel
- Milk carton
- Scissors and blunt table knife
  (for a grownup's use only)

## HERE'S WHAT YOU DO:

1. Use a hand shovel to dig a hole. Return some loose dirt and a handful of grass back into the hole. Add enough water to make the mixture moldable. Use your hands to make an even blend of soil, straw (or grass clippings), and water.

2. Have a grownup make a mold from a milk carton by cutting off the bottom, and the top plus ⅓ of the carton, so that only ⅔ of the walls remain.

3. Sprinkle a clear, sunny spot of ground with straw. Set the mold on top. Fill the mold right to the top with tightly packed adobe.

4. Use a blunt knife to cut between the adobe and the edge of the mold.

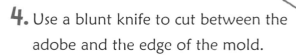

5. Carefully lift the mold and leave the brick in the sun to dry.

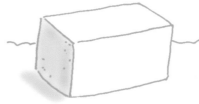

Down to Earth

# More to Explore

## Mini-Bricks

Fill an ice-cube tray with stiff adobe. Let the bricks dry hard over the course of several days.

## Round Bricks

Use a coffee can with the top and bottom removed as a mold. Fill partially with adobe, and lift off.

## Tall Wall

Let the bricks dry hard for several days. Set them out in a row using mortar (the same adobe mix) to hold them together. Make another row on top of the first.

## Let's Get Practical

**What makes adobe strong?** The word *adobe* means *clay* in Spanish. Since clay soil is so fine, it makes the best bricks. Water can surround each tiny soil particle like glue. The particles all stick together tightly, making a brick that won't crumble easily. Try the *More to Explore* experiments on page 85. Which one builds the strongest earth pie? Through similar testing over the years, people have found that adding straw (like grass clippings) to soil makes a stronger adobe brick. If you like getting into squishy mud with both hands, adobe brick-making is for you!

## What On Earth?

## For Thousands of Years, People All Over The World Have Used The Soil To Build Their Homes

We probably got the idea from animals. Beavers use soil to waterproof their dams. Termites find it makes cozy cone-shaped homes. Swallows build nests using grass and mud from nearby streams. It might take 1,000 bird-size mouthfuls of mud to build one nest! Some frogs raise their family in the protection of a mud wall at the edge of a pond. Water seeps in as the tadpole babies grow. By the time young frogs are strong enough to live on their own, the water has risen high enough to let them swim over the wall and into the pond.

**Read It!**
See clever animal homes in *And So They Build* by Bert Kitchen. Learn about people's homes around the world in *Houses and Homes* by Ann Morris.

# Rock Out!

Rocks are super to collect because they come in all sorts of interesting shapes and sizes. Geologists (scientists who study the earth) learn about rocks by comparing how rocks are *alike* and *different*. Be a geologist and organize a rock collection. How will you sort your rocks: by their color, size, shape, or some other way?

## Gather and Sort

**1.** Gather rocks from your backyard or near your home.

**2.** Wash the rocks in water. How do they change when wet?

**3.** Find a *round* rock. Can you find more? Find a *smooth* rock. Are there others? Sort similar rocks together in piles by *color*. Now sort by *size*, then by *shape*. Can you organize rocks in another way?

**4.** Line up rocks from biggest to smallest, heaviest to lightest, darkest to lightest, or smoothest to roughest.

Down to Earth

# Super Fun

## Play a Pebble Game

You and a friend gather about 20 pebbles each. Sit with your pile. Set out 5 very different-looking pebbles on bottle caps between you. (You need to keep track of these five.) The idea is to get rid of your pebbles by matching them to the ones in the middle. If you can think of a way one of your pebbles matches one of those five, set it in that pile and tell the other players why. Is it the same color, size, shape, or texture? Take turns matching.

**Critter Paperweights.** Pick a favorite rock. Does its shape remind you of a creature? Use acrylic paint to make a rock creature. Once dry, use it as a critter paperweight.

**Pebble Patterns.** Start a collection of favorite pebbles. Place them in interesting shapes, lines, and patterns.

**Rock Sounds.** Tap different rocks together. Compare the sounds they make. How do rocks sound when dropped on the sidewalk? Roll pebbles around in a metal pie plate. How do they sound?

**Rock Prints.** Dip rock faces (sides) into trays of tempera paint, and press onto paper. Why do you think the prints looks so different from the rocks?

## Helping Hands

Organizing information is a core science skill you can build by using familiar objects such as pebbles, leaves, and rocks from a child's own world.

**Read It!**

Do you have a favorite rock? Read *Everybody Needs a Rock* by Byrd Baylor. Just how important can a pebble be? Find out by reading *Alexander and the Wind-up Mouse* by Leo Lionni.

# Change IT!

Change is all around you. Day changes into night. Seeds change into plants. Ice changes into water. There are all sorts of ways things change. Here, you'll discover exciting changes you can create using ingredients right in your kitchen cabinet. Have you ever wondered how milk can change into ice cream or how flour, sugar, and butter can change into a cookie? Would you like to change sugary water into a sparkling necklace? Then start mixing up these exciting science-change concoctions!

## Very Important Note:

The mixtures in this chapter are made from items found in your kitchen, so you can eat some of them. But not all mixtures are edible, even if they are made from kitchen ingredients. So never eat concoctions you mix, unless a grownup says, "OK to eat!" In this book look for this symbol  which means "OK to eat!"

# Purple Cow

Change an ordinary glass of milk into an extraordinary drink. Can you predict how to make it purple and fruity?

## HERE'S WHAT YOU NEED:

- Milk
- Grape juice
- Drinking glass
- Stirring spoon

## HERE'S WHAT YOU DO:

**1.** Examine some milk and grape juice very carefully. What color is each? How does each one taste? Smell?

**2.** Predict what will happen if you mix them together. Then pour ⅔ cup (150 ml) milk and ⅓ cup (75 ml) grape juice into a glass. Stir. Taste the new drink. How is it like the milk and juice you started with? How is it different? Now which drink do you like best—milk, grape juice, or the combination Purple Cow?

## Science Talk

Purple Cow may be a delicious drink, but it also comes with a special scientific name. It's called a *solution*. Scientists use this word the describe liquids that mix together evenly. You learned that even though your new drink has a new taste, it's still a little like each of the ingredients it was made from.

# Super Fun

Mixing up a Purple Cow helped you discover that the new drink tastes a little like each of the ingredients it was made from. Be a scientist-chef by first predicting how each of the following drinks will taste. Then mix up the ingredients and see if you are right.

## Monkey Business

Guess an ingredient in Monkey Business. If you said, "banana," then you are right on! Add banana chunks to 1 cup (250 ml) of milk. Blend in a blender until smooth.

## Jungle Fizz

Add ½ cup (125 ml) cranberry juice to ½ cup (125 ml) lemon-lime soda. Taste. Add a scoop of vanilla ice cream to change this into a Jungle Fizz Float. It's delicious!

## Pucker Up

Mix 1 cup (250 ml) water with ¼ cup (50 ml) sugar. Add ½ cup (125 ml) freshly squeezed lemon juice.

## Purple Swirl

Swirl a tablespoon (15 ml) of frozen grape juice concentrate into a ½ cup (125 ml) of yogurt or soft ice cream.

## Invent Your Own

How could you make Orange Cow? Lemonade Fizz? Apple Swirl? Combine juices or add them to soda, milk, soft ice cream, or soft yogurt. Frozen fruits, juice concentrates, and sherbets are yummy additions. A grownup with a blender comes in handy for concocting delicious new drinks!

Change It!

# Sugar Crystal Necklaces

When you mix sugar and water together, it looks like the sugar is gone. Find out here if it has really disappeared.

## HERE'S WHAT YOU NEED:

- Bowl
- Sugar
- Warm water
- Pie plate
- String
- Waxed paper
- Spatula

## HERE'S WHAT YOU DO:

**1.** Mix sugar into very warm water until no more will dissolve. (The water looks clear and only a little sugar sinks to the bottom.)

**2.** Place strings along the bottom of a pie plate so that the ends dangle over the edge. Spoon the sugary water over the strings. The water should be very shallow in the pan.

**3.** Set a piece of waxed paper loosely on top of the pan. When the water is gone (evaporated into the air), use a spatula to lift out the strings. You've made sparkling sugar crystals you can eat!

## WHAT'S THE SOLUTION?

Mixing grape juice and milk makes a solution we call Purple Cow (page 94). Mixing sugar into water also makes a solution because the sugar dissolves. That means the sugar spreads evenly throughout the water, even though it seems to disappear. But did the sugar really vanish? Taste the new sugar-water solution and see. It's watery and sweet just like each of the ingredients it was made from. The sugar is still there!

# Sparkling Stars

Mix a special powder into water. Watch it disappear. Can you get the powder back out again? Wow! Observe the amazing change it makes!

**DO NOT EAT THIS!**

## HERE'S WHAT YOU NEED:

- Water
- Borax
- Jar
- Pipe cleaners
- String
- Paper clip

## HERE'S WHAT YOU DO:

**1.** Fill a wide-mouth jar with very warm water.

**2.** Mix borax into the water until it no longer disappears (dissolves) and only a little sinks to the bottom. Then you'll know you've mixed in as much borax as the water can hold, and you'll have a *solution* (see page 96).

**3.** Bend a pipe cleaner into a star or other interesting shape. Be sure it will fit into jar.

**4.** Tie a string to the top of the star. Tie a paper clip to the other end of the string. Push the star into the water, letting the string and clip hang over the outside of the jar.

**5.** How does the star look after a few hours? After sitting overnight? Carefully pull it out of the jar. Remember the borax you mixed into the water? What do you think made those sparkling crystals covering your star?

Change It!

97

# More To Explore

**DO NOT EAT THIS!**

## Creative Shape

Wind the pipe cleaner around your finger to make a spiral. Use several pipe cleaners to make a creature, tree, or flower shape.

## Ornament

Hang the star in front of a window. If it's Christmastime, hang it on your tree or if you made a Star of David, hang it up for Chanukah.

## Colored Crystals

Add a few drops of food coloring to your borax solution. Or use colored pipe cleaners. The colors will glow through the crystals.

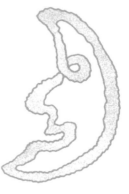

## More Speedy Sparklers

Instead of borax, have a grownup help you mix in Epsom salts or baking soda. How do these crystals compare?

## Helping Hands

**Is it a solution?** Set out a row of clear plastic cups of water. Kids predict which ingredients mix in water and which don't. Have children try adding sand, salt, instant drink mix, sugar, beans, pebbles, dirt, milk, and cooking oil. Let them predict and then observe results.

# Ice Cream in-a-Bag

If you cool liquids down, how do they change? *Explore* and *observe* how freezing changes your favorite drinks.

## HERE'S WHAT YOU NEED:

- 1 cup (250 ml) milk
- 2 tablespoons (30 ml) sugar
- ¼ cup (50 ml) salt
- Ice cubes
- 2 resealable sandwich bags
- Larger resealable bag
- Towel
- Plastic shopping bag
- Twist tie

## HERE'S WHAT YOU DO:

1. Add sugar and milk to the small resealable bag. Taste the solution. Let out some of the air as you zip to seal. Seal this bag inside another sandwich bag.

2. Place ice cubes in the bottom of the big bag. Add the small bag of milk and surround with more ice cubes. Sprinkle about ¼ cup (50 ml) of salt over the ice. Let out some of the air as you zip to seal.

3. Wrap a towel around the bag of ice. Place the bundle into a plastic shopping bag and seal with a twist tie.

4. Shake the bag. Have friends help you continue to shake for about 15 minutes. Remove the small bag and quickly rinse off the salt with cold water. Did the milk change? The ice cream you made is ready to enjoy!

## LeT'S GeT PRacTical

You probably noticed that ice cream from your bag-freezer is soft and light. Why? The shaking adds air to the ice cream. Machines keep the ice cream you buy moving as it freezes so there's enough air to make it soft enough to eat with a spoon.

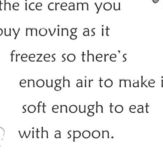

Change It!

# Cooking With The Sun

Want to discover how sun rays can change food? Well, first you've got to build a sun oven to catch those rays and put them to work. Test a marshmallow and observe the delicious results!

## HERE'S WHAT YOU NEED:

- Round-bottom thin plastic bowl or paper bowl
- Foil
- Twist tie
- Clear plastic wrap or bag
- Drinking straw
- Marshmallow
- Towel

## HERE'S WHAT YOU DO:

**1.** Line the bowl with foil. Smooth out the wrinkles and fold the foil over the edges so it hugs the sides.

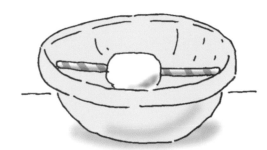

**2.** Skewer the marshmallow with the straw. Cut the straw and set in the bowl so that the marshmallow doesn't touch the foil.

**3.** Cover the bowl with clear plastic held on with a twist tie beneath the bowl.

**4.** Set the bowl facing the sun so that the sun lights the entire inside. Use a towel or pebbles to prop it up. (See next page.) Depending on how sunny it is, check back every 15–30 minutes. When the marshmallow feels very soft, it's ready to eat. Compare the taste and texture of a marshmallow right out of the bag with one right out of your cooker. What changed the marshmallow?

# More To Explore

Let the sun's rays do more of its magic on these foods. Can you predict the change? *Test and find out* if you are right by carefully setting these tidbits inside your sun oven:

- a large tortilla chip covered with shredded cheese
- a plain cookie covered with chocolate chips
- a pat of butter on a small piece of bread

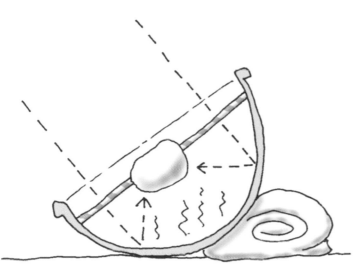

## Seems Like Magic!

Rays of sun pass through the plastic wrap and become trapped inside the oven. The shiny foil bounces, or reflects, the rays right at the marshmallow. The marshmallow makes a delicious change when it's hit by sun rays. It becomes very warm and mushy. Hard cheese and chocolate also change into a warm goo in the sun oven.

## What On Earth?

### An Oven on Wheels!

Park your car in the sun on a pleasant day. Come back in a few hours and, if you left the windows rolled up, it can feel as hot as an oven inside! Why? Your car works something like a sun oven. Rays of sun pass through the windows and become trapped. Everything inside the car, even the air, is warmer inside than outside. If you were unlucky enough to leave a candy bar in the car, observe the gooey change it made!

Change It!

101

# Super Fun
## Have a Sun Tea Party!

Fill a clear plastic jar with water. Take note of the water's temperature, color, and taste. Add several bags of herbal tea. Seal the lid, and set in the sun for a few hours. Now note the brew's temperature, color, and taste again. What made the water change? Cool and sweeten your tea by mixing it with cold fruit juice. Add ice cubes and invite friends to have a drink while sampling solar tidbits! What fun! If the sun's rays heat the water in your wading pool, you and your friends can have a wading party (with a grownup's supervision).

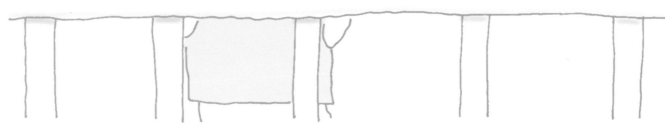

# Cookie Critters

From flour to dough to cookies, *explore* and *observe* the changes you can make by mixing and baking. How many science changes does it take to make cookie critters?

## HERE'S WHAT YOU NEED:

- 1 ¼ cups (300 ml) flour
- ¼ cup (50 ml) sugar
- ½ cup (125 ml)
- Soft butter or margarine
- ½ teaspoon (2 ml) vanilla
- Foil

## HERE'S WHAT YOU DO:

**1.** Blend the flour, sugar, butter, and vanilla together in a bowl. How is the dough different from the flour, sugar, or butter you started with? How is it the same? Use your sense of *smell*, *taste*, and *feel* to help you observe the changes.

**2.** Working on a piece of foil, mold the dough into a flat creature. Alligators, whales, turtles, fish, snakes, birds, and butterflies work well.

**3.** Carefully lift the foil with the critters onto a cookie sheet. Ask a grownup to help you bake the creatures at 300° F (150° C) for about 20 minutes. How are the baked creatures different from the unbaked dough? How are they different from each ingredient? Taste the differences. What do you think caused the changes?

*Change It!*

## Let's Get Practical

### Action Reaction

Bake the dough and you've made more than a cookie critter. You've made something special happen that scientists call a *chemical reaction*. By heating the dough, you changed it into something new. The cookie critter is very different from the butter, sugar, and flour you started with. Chemical changes are happening everywhere: nails rusting, marshmallows roasting, and cookies baking. *These are all chemical changes because something very new and different is being made!*

## Super Fun

### Color Your Critters

Add a few drops of food coloring to a handful of dough. Press and fold until it turns color. Make dough in a few colors. Try making creatures with spots, stripes, or different-colored body parts.

# Gooblek

How does cornstarch change when you add water? It becomes some wonderfully weird stuff, called Gooblek. The best way to explore Gooblek is by getting your hands into it. Is it a solid or a liquid? Is it wet? Is it dry? That's for you to decide.

**DO NOT EAT THIS!**

## HERE'S WHAT YOU NEED:

- Cornstarch
- Water
- Pan
- Mixing spoon

## HERE'S WHAT YOU DO:

**1.** Using a spoon, blend ¾ cup (175 ml) water with 1 ¼ cups (300 ml) of cornstarch in a pan.

**2.** Gooblek should be thick enough to form a ball by rolling it between your palms. Add more water or cornstarch, if needed. Stick your hand in the concoction. How does Gooblek feel? Wet or dry? Gently touch the pan of Gooblek. Now slap the surface. Squeeze some in your hand. When does it feel wet? When does it feel dry?

Change It!

105

# Explore and Observe

## Roll It

Form a ball by rolling Gooblek between your palms. What happens when you lift one hand away?

## Break It

Can you break a chunk of Gooblek in half?

## Slap It

Flatten the Gooblek in the pan. Slap it, and try to get the "liquid" to splash.

SPLAT!

## On or In?

Set objects of different weights in the pan of Gooblek. Do they stay on top or sink in?

## Color It

Divide Gooblek into three parts. Color one yellow, another blue, and another red. Mix spoonfuls of these colors together. What new colors can you make?

## Dry It

Leave a pan of Gooblek in the sun. What's left after a few hours? What happens when you add water?

**Read It!**

What if Gooblek fell from the sky? Read *Bartholomew and the Ooblek* by Dr. Seuss and see!

## What Is It?

Is Gooblek a solid or a liquid (see page 22)? You probably noticed that it acts like both! Why? Because tiny grains of cornstarch (a solid) don't dissolve in water (a liquid) like the sugar dissolves in water on page 96. Instead, the cornstarch stays separate and just floats.

PLEASE STAY AWAY FROM ME

So when you move the Gooblek slowly (tilting the pan, letting it ooze), *it flows more like a liquid*. When you move the Gooblek quickly (squeezing or slapping), *it acts more like a solid*.

## Saying Good-bye

**Say Good-bye to Gooblek . . . Safely!**

- Gooblek will clog drains. Do not pour it down the sink, and do not flush it down the toilet.
- It's only cornstarch, so yes, you can compost Gooblek.

- For a Gooblek supply, let the water dry out, and you've got cornstarch again. Store the dry granules of cornstarch in a resealable plastic bag. Add water to reuse on an "indoors" day.

COMPOST

## What On Earth?

### Corn Is a Wonder Plant!

Almost every part is useful. Enjoy the *kernels* right off the cob. Or grind them into *cornmeal* to make wonderful cereals, breads, and tortillas. The *cornstarch* in Gooblek is also used to make pudding and finger-paint nice and thick. *Corn oil* comes from the kernel. Even the *cobs* are used to feed farm animals. And the towering *cornstalks* can be made into paper! Next time you eat popcorn, think of the many other ways corn is important.

Change It!

# Super Fun
## Pool Party

If a grownup lets you fill a kiddy pool with Gooblek (outdoors only), you're a very lucky kid. Invite your friends over for a backyard Gooblek bash. Tiptoe through it. Does it squish? Set stuff on top of it. Do things sink? Hose down the mess when you're done.

# How's That Sound?

Sit quietly for a moment. What do you hear? Burgers sizzling on the stove? Footsteps pattering across the floor? The purring of your cat? What is sound? How does it travel from your cat to you? Learn about sound by making your own awesome sound makers. If you like to crash, bang, rattle, boom, or whisper secrets to a friend, you'll find lots of fun ahead.

# Whiz-Bang Gizmos

Sound is made when something vibrates or moves very quickly over and over again. When you hear a sound, something had to move. Make crazy sounds by getting gizmos vibrating in the most unusual ways.

ball and rub up and down the string. If you think this sounds like a chicken, decorate this gizmo to look like one! Paste on bits of paper for a beak, eyes, tail, and other details. Or use markers to make your own crazy creature.

## Hum

Decorate an empty toilet tissue roll. Punch a hole about an inch (2.5 cm) from one end. Secure a small piece of waxed paper over the other end of the roll with a rubber band. Hum or sing into the open end. How does it sound?

## Screech

Have a grownup help you thread about 20" (50 cm) of string through a small hole at the bottom of a paper cup. Attach a paper clip to the outside end so the string doesn't pull through. Now dampen your fingers or a cotton

## Warble

Thread a string through the pull tab of an empty soda can and knot it into a loop. Fill the can partway with water. Hold the loop while you bang on the can with a spoon. What do you hear?

# Bang

Fold a page of newspaper as shown in the two diagrams. Hold on to the long ends and whip it down sharply. Try using different kinds of paper. What do you think makes the sound?

# Plink

Stretch wide, medium, and skinny rubber bands across the opening of a small box. Pluck each one. Compare their sounds. If you can find different-sized bands to make high (3), middle (2), and low (1) sounds, you can play the song on page 112.

# Boom

Hold the scrunched neck of a paper lunch bag in your fist. Blow into the bag until it puffs up. Squeeze the neck shut, and use your other hand to slap the bag so it explodes. What do you hear?

FOLD 1  FOLD 1
FOLD 2
FOLD 1  FOLD 1

FOLD 4  FOLD 3  FOLD 5

HOLD HERE

SHOULD LOOK LIKE THIS

BANG!

How's That Sound?

## Ding, Ding, Ding

Find three tall glass bottles, all the same type. Fill one almost to the top, one midway, and add just a little water to the last. Play your bottle band by tapping each with a spoon or blowing across the top of each. Compare the sound each bottle makes. Notice that the high sound changes from least amount of water when tapping to most amount of water when blowing.

## What's The Buzz?

Sound is simply tiny back-and-forth movements called vibrations. They travel from the spot where the sound is made, through the air, and to your ear. How do you hear the buzz of a bee? The bee's wings move quickly back and forth, causing the nearby air to move back and forth, too. The vibrating air travels and shakes a part of your ear called the eardrum. Those vibrations become a message that goes to your brain to be figured out. It's as if your brain says, "That vibration is a bee buzzing. Watch out!" Can you find the vibrating part of each gizmo you made?

## Hot Cross Buns

Hot cross buns

   3    2    1

Hot cross buns

   3    2    1

One – a – pen – ny

  1   1   1   1

Two – a – pen – ny

  2   2   2   2

Hot cross buns

   3    2    1

*These bottles are filled for tapping—high (3) to low (1)

# See Sound

You can't really see sound, but here's a way to see what it does. Sound travels, and if it's powerful enough, it can actually move something in its path.

## HERE'S WHAT YOU NEED:

- ½ gallon (2 L) plastic ice cream or yogurt tub
- Clear plastic bag
- Safety scissors
- Large rubber band
- Crispy rice cereal
- Metal pan lid
- Mixing spoon

## HERE'S WHAT YOU DO:

**1.** Cut open the bag to make a plastic sheet. Pull it tightly over the top of the tub as your grown-up assistant secures it with a rubber band. Pull it so the drum skin is tight. Set crispy rice cereal on top.

**2.** Hold the lid close to the drum. Bang it sharply and rapidly with the spoon.

**3.** Look at the cereal. What do you observe? What do you think makes the cereal dance?

## Sound Waves?

Toss a pebble in a puddle. Notice the water's ripples spreading outward in circles from where the pebble landed. That's very much the way the vibrations spread outward from where a sound is made.

How's That Sound?

113

# More To Explore

## Make a Sound Cannon

Here's another way to see how sound travels. You can aim sound toward a streamer and make it wiggle!

**1.** Use rubber bands to tightly secure plastic to both ends of a paper tissue roll. Poke a hole in the plastic at one end.

**2.** Be sure both plastic skins are pulled tight. Have a friend hold a tissue paper streamer very still. Now face the hole toward the streamer. Tap on the other end. Can you make the streamer move with your tapping sounds?

**3.** Hold the cannon with the hole towards your face. Tap on the other end. Can you feel sound moving the air?

TAP TAP

**4.** Pull the plastic with the hole in it off the sound cannon. Speak into this open end. Place your fingers lightly on the plastic skin at the other end. Can you feel the vibrations?

**5.** Put your hand on the front of your throat. Speak. What do you feel?

## What On Earth?

### Insect Orchestra

Insects "play" their body parts to make the most unusual sounds. Grasshoppers do it by rubbing a leg against a wing. Crickets and katydids rub their wings together. The rough wing edges vibrate, and we hear chirping.

Cicadas rattle "drums" (little air spaces covered with skin) inside their bodies to make that special buzzing sound. Tiny insect bodies don't leave much space for ears. You might be surprised to learn that katydids have ears on their legs! A warm summer night is the best time to hear the concert!

# Trumpet Ear

Quiet sounds are hard to hear. Explore a way to make them louder. Give your ear a boost by making a giant trumpet ear!

## HERE'S WHAT YOU NEED:
- Construction paper
- Tape
- Safety scissors

## HERE'S WHAT YOU DO:

1. You'll want to make two trumpet ears. For each, roll a sheet of paper into a cone shape, very narrow at one end and wider at the other end. Hold it together with tape. Trim the wide end so that it's even.

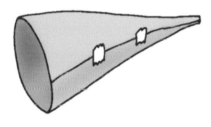

2. Sit still and listen to the room. Now "put on" your ears and listen to the difference.

**Read It!**
- *Crash! Bang! Boom!* and *Gobble, Growl, Grunt* by Peter Spier
- *City Sounds* by Craig Brown
- *Mr. Brown Can Moo, Can You?* by Dr. Seuss
- *Polar Bear, Polar Bear, What Do You Hear?* by Bill Martin, Jr.
- *What Can Pinky Hear?* By Lucy Cousins

How's That Sound?

# More To Explore

## Small Sound

Set a ticking watch on the table. Stand back from it. How well can you hear it? Now hold your trumpet ear with the wide end close to the watch and the narrow end to your ear. How does the sound change?

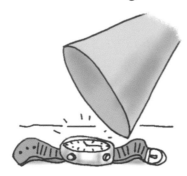

## Listen Up

Use your trumpet ear to hear:

- the whispers of your friend
- the purring of your cat
- a radio turned down very softly
- Have your friend lie down. Place the wide part firmly on his or her chest. Be very quiet and you'll hear a heart beating!

## Megaphone

Flip the ear trumpet around, and you've got a megaphone. Speak into the narrow end of the megaphone and ask your friend to listen. Have him or her compare your voice with and without the megaphone. **Note: Never shout through a megaphone close to someone's ear.**

## Super Sound

What do you *predict* will happen if you use a trumpet ear and a megaphone at the same time? *Guess, test, and find out.* Have your friend stand a few feet away, and face his or her trumpet ear at your megaphone. Whisper, talk softly, and make strange sounds. Take turns. How do your voices change?

## Let's Get Practical

### Hear Small Sounds

Sound waves spread out and become harder to hear as they travel. But your megaphone gathers them together to make your voice more powerful. Your friend's trumpet ear collects the vibrations and directs them into his or her ear. Together, the trumpet ear and megaphone can make small sounds seem big.

## What On Earth?

## Rabbit Ears

Why does the rabbit need those huge ears? The better to hear with, of course! Just like the trumpet ear you made, rabbit ears are very helpful for collecting sounds. Rabbits can also point their ears all around, so they can be constantly listening for sounds of danger coming from all directions. Being able to hear a coyote softly rustling dry grass gives the rabbit the chance it needs to hop away and protect itself.

# Party Line

Speak to a friend and you set sound-waves moving through the air. But can sound travel through something solid like a wall or string? *Guess, test, and find out* by talking to your friends on this special telephone.

## HERE'S WHAT YOU NEED:

- Two 15 feet (4.5 m) long pieces of string
- 4 plastic yogurt cups

## HERE'S WHAT YOU DO:

**1.** Ask a grownup to poke one small hole in the bottom of each of the four yogurt cups. Attach a cup to each end of the strings. Push the end through the hole from the outside and knot it inside the cup to keep it from slipping back out.

**2.** Connect the two strings by knotting them tightly together at their centers.

**3.** *Now try it out!* Have a friend hold each cup. Spread out so the strings are tight and you form an "X" shape. Take turns whispering and listening into the cups.

## Good Vibrations

Sounds are simply vibrations. Your telephone is a vibration-collecting gizmo. That's why it works so well! Your friend speaks into his or her cup and gets it vibrating. The cup vibrates the string and the string vibrates your cup. All those vibrations let you hear your friend's soft whisper. What happens when you loosen the string? You lose an important vibrating connection, and you can't hear a word!

How's That Sound?

# More To Explore

- How many lines or kids can you add to your phone system? How few can use the phones?

- Make telephones with different cups: paper, hard plastic, soft plastic, cans. Compare the sounds.

- Let the strings hang loose. Make them tight. Compare the sounds.

- Pluck the string or tap the cup instead of talking.

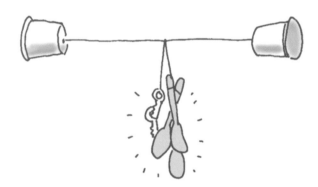

- Tie metal spoons or keys on either end of a string. Drape this string over the phone line string and let the objects dangle. How do they sound through the phone line as they clank together?

## Can Sound Travel Along a Wall?

You and a friend stand at either end of a solid wall. Listen while your friend knocks on the wall. Now put your ear against the wall while your friend knocks. Compare the sounds.

## Can Sound Travel Through a Tube?

You and a friend hold onto either end of a dry garden hose and stretch it out. Take turns whispering and listening through the long air tube. Whisper and listen without the tube at the same distance away. Compare the sounds.

# Super Fun

## Fly Footsteps

Capture a fly or other small critter in a paper cup. Use a rubber band to hold a small sheet of waxed paper over the opening. Put the cup near your ear and listen carefully. Each little footstep vibrates the cup, so you can actually hear the fly walking!

## Doctor, Doctor

If you've ever visited the doctor, you've probably seen a stethoscope. Just as the garden hose (page 118) lets you hear whispers, the stethoscope is made to carry the quietest sounds to the doctor's ears. Part of the device is placed on your back to pick up the tiny sound vibrations of your heart and lungs. Instead of the sound spreading out every which way, it stays within narrow tubes that are plugged directly into the doctor's ears so hardly any sound is lost.

How's That Sound?

# Shake and Rattle Game

Good scientists use all their senses to observe. Hone your sense of hearing by playing a matching game for your ears!

## HERE'S WHAT YOU NEED:

Sound-making stuff like paper clips • washers • beads • buttons • coins • beans • peas • rice • sugar • pebbles • Styrofoam • marbles • water

## HERE'S WHAT YOU DO:

**1.** Fill pairs of film canisters with sound-making stuff. Snap on the lids. Shake. Which sounds are loud, soft, scratchy, clanky?

**2.** Set out about five pairs of shakers. Add an empty pair for fun. Mix them up. Now take turns with a friend. First shake a shaker. You have three chances to find the matching sound. If you find the match, keep the pair and take another turn. The winner is the player with the most pairs. To play cooperatively, together try to match all the mixed-up pairs of shakers.

## More To Explore

### Go on a Sound Search

Listen carefully for sounds inside your home, in your backyard, at different times of day, in a paper cup. (Place a cup over one ear and your hand over your other ear.)

### Make Your Own Sound Safari

Using a wooden spoon, gently tap on objects such as furniture, walls, floor, toys, trees, your car, and bushes in your yard.

# MoVe IT!

Motion is all about getting from one place to another. It's about changing position. People can move themselves, but they also invent things that can move. You can wiggle your thumb, and you've probably seen a huge fire truck whizzing down the road. Big or little—it's all movement! Try some movement now with your body. Twirl, hop, somersault, or jump. Balance on one foot or roll down a gentle hill. You can make toys that also move in different ways. Play with them and explore marvelous motion!

# RoLLer Derby

Make a ramp and put objects on a roll. Does everything move the same way or do some things move crooked, straight, fast, or slow? Can you *predict* the ones that will roll the farthest? Test them to see if you are right!

## HERE'S WHAT YOU NEED:

- Cookie sheet
- Books
- Rolling objects: marbles, balls, fruits, toys, cans, and more!

## HERE'S WHAT YOU DO:

1. Create a ramp by placing one end of a cookie sheet on a stack of books on the floor.

2. You and your friend each have 5 minutes to gather 8 different objects that you predict will make good rollers (toy car, pebble, ball, orange, cardboard tube).

3. Each of you rolls an object down the ramp, noting where it stops. The object that rolls the farthest wins that turn. The winner is the player with the most far-rolling objects.

# More To Explore

## Test All Sorts of Rollers

### Veggie Rollers

Roll fruits and vegetables—such as carrots, bananas, oranges, grapes, and cabbage heads—down the ramp. Predict which will roll the farthest. Were you right?

### Small Rollers

Collect small objects that you predict will make good rollers, such as pebbles, marbles, twigs, and paper clips.

## Test All Sorts of Sliders

How do objects slide down the ramp? Test objects you predict will make good sliders, such as blocks, a book, paper clip, rock, eraser, and stuffed toy. How about an ice cube?

### Read It!

Read *Mama Zooms* by Jane Cowen-Fletcher to discover how a mother and child roll all around town! *Freight Train and Truck* by Donald Crews offer fast-rolling fun, too. See how folks all over the world move from here to there in *On the Go* by Ann Morris.

Move It!

123

# Super Fun

## Crazy Creatures

How does an orange roll? A lemon? An apple? Turn these weird rollers into crazy creatures. Decorate a 9" (22.5 cm) square of tissue paper with spots, stripes, eyeballs, or any other pictures or patterns. Twist the corners of the square to form the paper into a cap shape. Set the cap on top of a lemon you've placed on a smooth, hard floor. Now kick it gently with your toe. Just watch your creature wobble and bob across the floor!

## Drawing Conclusions

What do you notice about your best rollers? You've likely discovered that *round* objects work best. Now compare a marble to a grape. *Heavy* objects also go farther. A *smooth* ball will likely travel farther than a *rough* orange the same size and weight. Compare a marble with a melon. Marbles win almost every time; they're smooth, round, and heavy for their size. That's what it takes to be a super roller!

## Helping Hands

Help kids turn observations into conclusions by asking them to identify characteristics of rollers that travel farthest. Compare winners from different groups so an overall winner begins to emerge. Ask, "Between the marble, grape, and orange, which goes farthest?"

# FLipping ELf

Make air powerful enough to give an elf the push she needs to somersault. An empty liquid dishwashing detergent bottle is perfect for testing the power of squeezed air. Squeeze the bottle with your hands and begin experimenting!

## HERE'S WHAT YOU NEED:

- Lightweight paper
- Safety scissors
- Tape
- Empty detergent bottle with open lid on

## HERE'S WHAT YOU DO:

1. Use a sheet of lightweight paper to make a paper elf. Roll into a cone for the body. Decorate it with marking pens. Tape on paper arms and legs.

2. Set your elf gently on the top of an empty, dry detergent bottle. What do you think will happen when you squeeze the bottle?

Move It!

125

# More To Explore

- Squeeze the bottle quickly. Squeeze it slowly. Don't squeeze it at all. What's the difference?

- Take off the lid so the opening is larger. Set the elf on top and squeeze. Does the elf move differently?

- Make different-sized elves. Use different types of squeeze bottles. How does the flipping action change?

Wheee !!

# Super Fun

## Water Power

**A burst of air can flip an elf. What do you predict a burst of water might do? Make a target game and see!**

Two connected walls of a milk carton make fine targets. Set them upright, and fill an empty detergent bottle with water. Aim your squeeze bottle. Can you use a spurt of water to knock the targets over? What happens when you change the size of the bottle's opening? Compare the way water moves when squeezed out of the bottle with the lid off and with the lid on.

# Quicker and Stronger

The more quickly you squeeze the bottle, the more quickly the air moves out. Speedy air has the strength to make things, like your elf, move. But something else adds to the speed of the air.

**Air moves quickly when it's forced through a small hole.** That's just what you did when you squeezed air out of the bottle and through the tiny hole in the lid. Zoom—the little elf flipped! What happened when you took off the lid and made the hold larger? Not much action. **Try this:** Hold a piece of paper upright in front of you face. Blow on it with your mouth wide open. Now pucker your lips and blow again. Compare how the paper moves each time.

## What On Earth?

### Can Air Hold Up a Car?

You bet, if that air is squashed inside the tires! Have you ever watched someone pump up the tire of a car or bike? They're filling that tire with air—more and more air. So much air is squashed inside that it tries to push its way out. But it can't, unless there's a hole. So the air pushes hard against the inside walls of the tire instead. The tire feels hard and firm. It's strong enough to hold you when you're riding your bike—or even strong enough to hold a car.

Move It!

127

# Super Spinners

From yo-yos to egg beaters to the water whirling down the tub drain to the earth we stand on, spinning motion is everywhere! Explore that motion as you make your own super spinners. Your goal is to *experiment*; then *create* a top that spins for a long, long time.

## HERE'S WHAT YOU NEED:

- Smooth-edged lid from a 12 ounce (342 ml) frozen juice can
- Pencil
- Cereal box cardboard
- Safety scissors
- Pushpin
- Round toothpick

## HERE'S WHAT YOU DO:

**1.** Trace around a frozen juice lid on to cereal box cardboard. Cut the circle out. Stick a pushpin through the center. Then push a round toothpick through the hole. Can you spin this top?

**2.** Experiment to see what makes it spin for a long time. Make a short tip by pushing just a little of the toothpick through the hole. Make a long tip by pushing most of the toothpick though. Make another cardboard circle and put the hole away from the center. How does it spin? Try spinning a square- or triangle-shaped top. Compare the spins and wobbles. Which top spins for the longest time?

# More To Explore

## Spinners Galore

You probably discovered that a circle-shaped top with a hole right through the center works best. Also, a top with a short tip and a long handle was less likely to fall over! Use what you learned to "invent" the best super spinner.

**Ask a grownup to help you poke pencils through the center of:**

- plastic yogurt container lids
- different-sized paper plates
- margarine tubs
- different-sized cardboard circles made by tracing around lids and bowls.

**Tip:** First make the hole with a pushpin.

## Art in Motion

Draw colorful patterns on cardboard circles. Compare how the patterns and colors look when they're still with how they look while spinning.

**Try your own designs or these:**

- a spiral that starts in the center
- a bull's-eye with each band a different color
- divide the circle into different-colored pie slices
- try other color combos

Move It!

# More To Explore

## Top Tracks

Push a felt-tip marker through a hole in the center of a 1 quart (1 L) yogurt container lid. Spin the top on a piece of paper to capture its "tracks." Try spinning different-colored pens.

# Super Fun

## Be a Spinner

Twirl around. Hold newspaper streamers in your hands as you let your arms hang loose at your sides. Observe what happens to your arms and streamers as you spin.

# What On Earth?

## Salad Spinner Art

Set a circle of paper or a small paper plate in the bottom of an old salad spinner. Spoon different colors of paint on the paper. Set the lid on the spinner and spin! **Wow!**

## Soggy Salad?

Without a kitchen salad spinner, your salad might be soggy! How does this gizmo work? (Holding streamers while twirling gives you a clue.) Just like the spinning paint, the streamers flew outward, and so does the water on the salad leaves. Look inside the salad spinner and you'll see a basket with plenty of holes in its side walls. The spinning water moves outward, right off those leaves and out those holes. Try it and see!

## Be a Spin Detective!

- What spinners can you find around your home (dryer, blender, salad spinner)? Now look outdoors (bicycle and car wheels, roller skates, Frisbee).

- Have you ever spun an egg? How does it spin if it's hard-boiled? Raw? Do you think you could sort out the boiled eggs for breakfast by doing a spin test?

- Find things around the house you think might spin: coins, lids, balls. Which make the best spinners?

Move It!

# Balancing Act

Lift one leg off the ground. Now stand on your tip-toes. Do you feel wobbly? How can you keep yourself from tumbling over? Your body predicts what it needs to do to keep you upright. Did you notice your leg or arms come shooting out to help you keep your balance? *Explore* what makes objects wobble. Can you predict how to make them come back in place? *Test* your guess by giving it a try.

## Be a Balancing Act!

Stand on one foot. Twist your body around. Can your arms keep you from falling over? Can you stand on your head? Try standing sideways on one hand and one foot. Can you stand on your tip-toes? How do you feel most wobbly? Which position feels most stable?

# Tumbling Toys

Make a toy tower by stacking blocks, cars, stuffed animals, balls, anything! How high can you go? Which toy shapes stack best? Play this as a game. You lose if your addition makes the tower fall over! Now try to re-stack the same toys but in a new order. See if you can make a higher stack!

# FingerTip Fun

What can you balance on your fingertip? Try a ruler. Put your finger under different numbers. Under what number does the ruler balance best?

**Here are fun objects to try to balance:**

- Frisbee
- Clothes hanger
- Ball
- Book
- Sunglasses

Keep moving them around on your finger until you find the place each will balance. What shape works best?

**Read It!**
Read books by Emily Arnold McCully about a little girl who loves to balance: *Mirette on the High Wire* and *Starring Mirette and Bellini.*

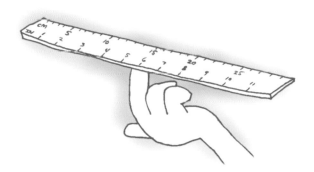

Move It!

## Balancing Box

Hide a full can of soup in the corner of a shoe box. Now set the box on a tabletop so that the empty part hangs far out over the edge. Only the part with the can needs to be on the table. Put on the lid. Can you amaze grownups with your box?

## Tower Power

Make your own building set. Use a stack of paper or plastic party cups all the same size. Ask a grownup to help you cut large panels from cereal and cracker boxes. Make tall towers by layering upside-down cups and cardboard panels. How high can you build?

# Let's Get Practical

**Drop a ball. Where does it go? Push yourself up high in a swing. What makes the swing fall back down?** Gravity is the force that pulls everything down toward the ground. So how can you keep gravity from pulling down your block tower? As you build, you're deciding where to put the next block so that the tower stays put. Things *balance*, or keep form toppling over, when their weight is arranged just right.

# Helping Hands

From building block towers to walking on low walls, young children constantly experiment with the physics of balance. Manipulating the weight of a variety of objects gives children insight into the laws of stability. Let intuition be their guide.

# See-Saw

If your playground has a see-saw, you and your friends can experiment with balance. Where can you sit so that the see-saw goes back and forth evenly? What makes one friend get stuck high in the air? What happens when you and your friend are perfectly balanced?

Move It!

# Index

Index

Index

# More Good Books from Williamson Books

Williamson Books are available from your bookseller or directly from Ideals Publications. Please see last page for contact and ordering information.

## Little Hands® Books for Ages 2 to 7:

*Parent's Guide Children's Media Award*
**Alphabet Art**
With A to Z Animal Art
& Finger Plays
BY JUDY PRESS

*Parents' Choice Recommended Award*
**Animal Habitats!**
Learning About North American
Animals and Plants through Art,
Science, and Creative Play
BY JUDY PRESS

**Around-the-World Art & Activities**
Visiting the 7 Continents
through Craft Fun
BY JUDY PRESS

**Art Starts for Little Hands!**
Fun & Discoveries for
3- to 7-year-olds
BY JUDY PRESS

**Creating Clever Castles & Cars**
(From Boxes and Other Stuff)
Kids Ages 3–8 Make Their Own
Pretend Play Spaces
BY MARI RUTZ MITCHELL

*Parents' Choice Recommended*
**Early Learning Skill-Builders**
Colors, Shapes, Numbers & Letters
BY MARY TOMCZYK

*Parents' Choice Gold Award*
**Fun with My 5 Senses**
Activities to Build Learning Readiness
BY SARAH. A. WILLIAMSON

*Parents' Choice Honor Award*
**Kids Create!**
Art & Craft Experiences for
3- to 9-Year-Olds
BY LAURIE CARLSON

**Kindergarten Success**
Helping Children Excel
Right from the Start
BY JILL FRANKEL HAUSER

*Parent's Guide Classic Award*
*LifeWorks Magazine Real Life Award*
**The Little Hands Art Book**
Exploring Arts & Crafts
with 2- to 6-year-olds
BY JUDY PRESS

**The Little Hands Big Fun Craft Book**
Creative Fun for 2- to 6-Year Olds
BY JUDY PRESS

*Parents' Choice Approved*
**Little Hands Create!**
Art & Activities for Kids
Ages 3 to 6
BY MARY DOERFLER DALL

*Parents' Choice Approved*
**Little Hands Paper Plate Crafts**
Creative Art Fun for
3- to 7-Year-Olds
BY LAURA CHECK

*American Bookseller Pick of the Lists*
**Math Play!**
80 Ways to Count & Learn
BY DIANE MCGOWAN & MARK SCHROOTEN

**Sing! Play! Create!**
Hands-On Learning for
3- to 7-Year-Olds
BY LISA BOSTON

## Kids Can!® Books for Ages 7 to 14:

*Parents' Choice Recommended*
**Making Amazing Art!**
40 Activities Using the
7 Elements of Art Design
BY SANDI HENRY

**The Kids' Multicultural Art Book**
Art & Craft Experiences
from Around the World
BY ALEXANDRA MICHAELS

*Parents' Choice Approved*
**The Kids' Multicultural Craft Book**
35 Crafts from
Around the World
BY ROBERTA GOULD

*Parents' Choice Approved*
*Skipping Stones Multicultural Honor Award*
*Benjamin Franklin Best Multicultural Book Award*
**The Kids' Multicultural Cookbook**
Food & Fun Around the World
BY DEANNA F. COOK

# Visit Our Website!

To see what's new with Williamson Books and Ideals Publications and learn more about specific titles, visit our website at: www.idealsbooks.com.

## To Order Books:

You'll find Williamson Books at your favorite bookstore, or you can order directly from Ideals Publications. We accept Visa and MasterCard (please include the number and expiration date).

**Order on our secure website: www.idealsbooks.com**

**Toll-free phone orders with credit cards: 1-800-586-2572**

**Toll-free fax orders: 1-888-815-2759**

Or send a check with your order to:
**Ideals Publications**
**Williamson Books Orders**
**2636 Elm Hill Pike, Suite 120**
**Nashville, Tennessee 37214**

Catalog request: web, mail, or phone

Please add **$4.00** for postage for one book plus **$1.00** for each additional book. Satisfaction is guaranteed or full refund without questions or quibbles.

143